Disruption, Disaster, and Death

HELPING STUDENTS DEAL WITH CRISES

FESTUS E. OBIAKOR
TERESA A. MEHRING
JOHN O. SCHWENN

Published by The Council for Exceptional Children

Library of Congress Cataloging-in-Publication Data

Obiakor, Festus E.
    Disruption, disaster, and death : helping students deal with crises /
Festus E. Obiakor, Teresa A. Mehring, John O. Schwenn.
        p. cm.
    Includes bibliographical references (p. 103).
    ISBN 0-86586-289-3
    1. School psychology–United States.   2. Crisis intervention
(Psychiatry)–United States.   3. Death–Psychological aspects.
I. Mehring, Teresa A.   II. Schwenn, John O.   III. Title.
LB1027.55.035   1996
371.4'6–dc21   96-40939
                                                                    CIP

LB
1027.55
.035
1997

ISBN 0-86586-289-3

Stock No. P5190

Printed in the United States of America

10   9   8   7   6   5   4   3   2   1

To

students

families

educators

and

community members

who have

come out

of

crises

stronger

and

wiser

Contents

CHAPTER 4: DEATH

CHAPTER 5: PREPARING GENERAL AND SPECIAL EDUCATORS FOR CRISES

PROLOGUE

In the words of a great American poet, "the times they are a changin" and this time, the change may not be easy. Teaching in today's schools becomes more challenging every day. Two key areas that make teaching increasingly difficult are dealing with the increasing occurrences of significant life tragedies and mastering and using collaborative techniques to address multidimensional problems that confront students.

Today's teachers are faced with more critical problems in their classrooms than ever before in history and this provides teachers with continuing and different opportunities and challenges (Obiakor, 1994; Schwenn, 1994; Ysseldyke & Algozzine, 1995). Making decisions about what to teach and how to teach it to students is increasingly complicated because of their different gender; race; ethnicity; language spoken at home; physical, mental, and emotional skill levels; parental income level; activity level; parental education; background experience; and family structure. These variations have a direct and significant impact on what general and special educators do to promote learning and student performance.

Today's teachers are also faced with significant, sudden or unanticipated events that result from or create a risk for serious personal injury (Mehring, 1995). Unauthorized entry by uninvited people, riots and protests, family quarrels spilling over into classrooms or school buildings, weapons on campus, and bomb threats are a few examples of *disruption* creating crises that can seriously influence instructional opportunities and teaching. Natural *disaster* (such as fires, earthquakes, and severe weather) and natural or accidental personal losses due to the *death* of a classmate, peer, teacher, parent, family member, friend, or other people are additional types of crises that general and special educators are increasingly having to prepare for in today's schools. Information on developing and using intervention strategies for addressing life's crises (e.g., disruption, disaster, and death) should be on the reading list of every general and special education teacher, administrator, counselor, and parent.

In this book, Obiakor, Mehring, and Schwenn provide general and special educators with a variety of very useful strategies for helping students deal with the crises that are becoming more and more common in their lives. From descriptions of plans for designing and using *Crisis Intervention Teams* dealing with critical events affecting faculty, staff, and students to a set of tips for defusing and debriefing students and staff members following a tragic event, this book provides a wealth of practical information for school personnel and other professionals faced with living with children and helping them cope with today's complex and, too often, difficult life experiences. I hope occasions seldom occur when I will need this book, but I am glad to know it exists and is so well done. I strongly urge readers to take advantage of it. As the popular ad goes, "Do not leave home without it!"

Bob Algozzine
Professor, Teaching Specialties
University of North Carolina, Charlotte

PREFACE

We started conceptualizing ideas for this book about three years ago when a Kansas man killed his parents and carried the mother's corpse in the trunk of his car to New York. Since then, many outrageous crimes have been committed, some in the remotest parts of this nation. Coupled with these senseless crimes are natural and unnatural disasters (e.g., floods, fires, and earthquakes) that have placed tremendous burdens on students, teachers, and communities. These crimes and disasters have disruptive effects on children and youth, especially those with exceptionalities.

Our initial goal was to write on the general topic of crisis intervention for atypical students. We found later that this gave us no pedagogical direction to address the myriad of disruptions, disasters, and deaths that confront students, parents, teachers and other professionals. But for the sophisticated editorial suggestions of Jean Boston and the Council for Exceptional Children staff, we would have remained in a quandary. It was a wise suggestion to title this book, *Disruption, Disaster, and Death: Helping Students Deal with Crises.* We are glad we listened!

The sad picture of life crises (such as disruption, disaster, and death) that confront America's children and youth is presented in Chapter 1 and throughout the book. In Chapter 2, we delve into disruption and intervention strategies to deal with disruption. Chapter 3 explores varying disasters and intervention strategies to address their after effects. In the same vein, Chapter 4 describes death-related crises and their intervention strategies. In Chapter 5, we summarize impacts of disruption, disaster, and death and preparations that general and special educators should have to adequately intervene when they occur. Each chapter contains a section addressing the needs of learners with exceptionalities. Additionally, each chapter has five discussion questions for practitioners. It is our hope that these questions would allow practitioners to apply, analyze, synthesize, and evaluate ideas already presented in the text.

We found writing this book intriguing and challenging. In our research of the issues, we discovered a dearth of innovative ideas and techniques for today's general and special educators. Sadly, as we were putting finishing touches to this book, one of us lost his father (Chief Charles O. Obiakor, Nze Agbako I of Obodoukwu, Nigeria). This very sad news became an inspiration to all of us. In the end, we put together the first comprehensive package of crisis intervention ideas and techniques for general and special educators.

We thank our families, colleagues, and friends for their support in this worthy venture. We also thank The Council for Exceptional Children staff for understanding the urgency of a book of this kind. Finally, we thank Bob Algozzine and Bridgie Ford for writing the Prologue and Epilogue of this book, respectively.

Festus E. Obiakor
Teresa A. Mehring
John O. Schwenn

CHAPTER 1

CHILDREN AND YOUTH IN CRISES

Historically, attempts to prevent crises from occurring at school or home have concentrated on evacuation procedures such as fire and natural disaster drills. Today's general and special educators and school staff face a much broader range of crises that cluster into three categories: disruption, disaster, and death. According to Pitcher and Poland (1993), most educators will face challenges associated with shootings, kidnappings, emotionally out of control staff members, and/or assaults on teachers at some point during their careers. As Riley (1993) points out:

- Approximately 3 million thefts and violent crimes occur on or near school campuses every year. This equates to nearly 16,000 incidents per school day, or one incident every 6 seconds.

- Approximately one of every five high school students now carries a firearm, knife, razor, club, or other weapon on a regular basis. Many of them carry these weapons to school.

- During a recent school year, approximately 20% of all public school teachers reported being verbally abused, and 8% reported being physically attacked. (p. 2)

It is relatively easy to recognize the many pressures and challenges that cause disruption, disaster, and death in today's society. Naturally occurring events and circumstances also have the potential to dislodge normal daily activities. While these pressures and events range from minor irritants to major disasters, the chances of these problem situations occurring on school grounds, during school time, or to students and staff have become a statistical probability in both rural and urban areas. About a decade ago, Gordon (1985) estimated that 1,000 teens attempt suicide each day. Around the same period, Vidal (1986) estimated that approximately 5,000 fifteen- to twenty-four-year-olds commit suicide each year. Similarly, Leder (1987) noted that the second highest cause of death amongst teenagers is suicide, and Meemot and Stone (1989) reported that every day one child is killed and ten injured in accidental shootings. Since then, youth homicide has doubled, and child and adolescent suicide rates have witnessed dramatic increases. The data provided by the Children's Defense Fund (1994) paint a very sad picture of America's children. This organization reports that each day

- 13 children die from guns.
- 30 children are wounded from guns.
- 202 children are arrested for drug offenses.
- 307 children are arrested for crimes of violence.
- 1,340 teenagers have babies.
- 2,255 teenagers drop out of school.
- 5,703 teenagers are victims of violent crime.

For many students with exceptionalities and their parents who already face additional challenges, life crises such as disruption, disaster, and death can be devastating, especially when general and special educators are unprepared or ill-prepared to deal with them (Morgan, 1994). The question is: How can school programs intervene in crisis situations without destroying the school culture? Three types of crises (disruption, disaster, and death) are discussed in this book, and guidelines are presented on how general and special educators must be prepared to foster stability in the school's general culture.

CRISES: MEANINGS AND IMPACTS

Jones and Patterson (1992) define a crisis as "a sudden, generally unanticipated event that profoundly and negatively affects a significant segment of the school population and often involves serious injury or death" (p. 8). Crises affecting school personnel, students, and parents can be grouped under disruption, disaster, and death. These events frequently affect people's physical or emotional well-being and, in turn, impact the school population. For students with exceptionalities, these events can have extreme, devastating effects, especially if and when their caretakers are affected or lack preparation.

Ironically, what is considered to be a crisis in one school setting may have minimal impact in another setting. Jones and Patterson (1992) explain that

> In a school of 4,000, a student's death may affect only his/her class or grade level team. In a student body of 300, that same death may be a significant crisis—especially if the community is one of closeknit and interrelated families. The identity of students affected also can influence the response, as can the degree of drama in the event. A lethal crash or drive-by shooting witnessed by students at school will create significantly more ripples than the same occurrence far from the school during vacation. (p. 8)

Consider the following school-related incidents which have each impacted upon students, teachers, parents, and their communities.

1. May 1986: An entire elementary school was taken hostage by a couple armed with several guns and a homemade bomb in Cokeville, Wyoming. Crowding 150 people into one classroom, the couple held the school hostage for 2 hours before the bomb was accidentally detonated setting the room and everyone in it on fire. Although no loss of life occurred, many students and staff members were badly burned.

2. December 1988: An automobile accident claimed the lives of four students from Molalla High School, Molalla, Oregon.

3. January 1989: A man carrying an AK-47 semiautomatic assault rifle walked onto an elementary school playground in Stockton, California, and opened fire. Less than 5 minutes later, five children and the gunman were dead; 29 other students and their teacher were wounded, 15 seriously.

4. February 1989: A fire razed almost the entire Baker High School, Baker, Oregon. The fire was caused by an overheated pipe in the air-handling unit above the ceiling and caused significant damage. No personal injuries occurred because of the preparedness of the staff.

5. November 1993: A 10-year-old boy was playing with his father's gun at home and accidentally shot himself. Several hours later, he died

from the gunshot wound. Students, teachers, and administrators in the Stillwell, Kansas, elementary school were stunned.

6. December 1993: Two preteen girls were abducted from St. Louis, Missouri neighborhoods, one walking to school, the other walking to a friend's house to help set up holiday lights. The bodies of both girls were discovered in abandoned areas about one week after each abduction. Shock, fear, and panic spread throughout each girl's school of attendance and other schools in the greater metropolitan area.

7. May 1995: The Federal Building in Oklahoma City, Oklahoma, was bombed killing more than 160 people including young children who attended a day care center located in the building. The nature of the crime devastated many families and disrupted the nation's equilibrium.

8. July 1996: TWA flight #800 en route to Paris, France exploded in the air, killing all passengers and crew aboard, including most of the French Club from a small-town high school in Pennsylvania. Everybody in the town at least knew somebody on that flight, and indeed, this disastrous accident disrupted many families, schools, communities, states, the nation, and the world. In addition, it left many unanswered questions for governmental agencies (e.g., the Federal Aviation Agency, the Federal Bureau of Investigation, the Central Intelligence and the National Transportation Safety Board).

Apparently, the number of crises affecting students, schools, and communities has spiraled upward. It has become extremely important for school staff members, teachers, and administrators to make advance plans for dealing with crisis situations. As Jones and Patterson (1992) indicate, "a school that is prepared before a crisis occurs will be much more likely to deal with students and staff effectively. An unprepared school is asking for chaos" (p. 11). There seems to be no easy solutions to the broad array of potential and real crises impacting students, schools, parents, and communities. Intervention plans should be developed and implemented by school districts and individual schools to assist administrators, teachers, staff members, students, parents, and community members to respond in an organized rather than disoriented fashion during and after disruption, disaster, and death. While crises may be unavoidable, swift and concerted actions by school authorities and community leaders can reduce or eliminate some potentially negative consequences.

As indicated earlier, what is crisis to a person, school, or community might be viewed and handled differently by another person, school, or community. But, for the purposes of this book, we discuss crises under the broad categories of disruption, disaster, and death. These categories present this book's basis for explanations of constructs, terminologies, and intervention techniques.

Disruption

Disruption includes any unauthorized event that would significantly impact the normal, daily school routine or the population of the school. Specific examples include (a) unauthorized entry by persons; (b) riots, protests, or walk-outs; (c) separation of parents or quarrels at home; (d) divorce of parents; (e) unlawful assemblies and gang-related activities; (f) sexual harassment and abuse, molestation, or rape; (g) hostage situations; (h) weapons-assault and shooting; and (i) bomb threats and hate crimes.

Disaster

Disaster is defined as a calamity or catastrophe brought about by a natural occurrence, mechanical malfunction, or utility disfunction of the facility. This type of crisis may range from minor inconveniences to catastrophic property or personal injuries and loss of life. Events that would lead to a disaster include (a) broken pipes; (b) loss of air conditioning; (c) loss of heat; (d) loss of other utility services; (e) hazardous material spillage or lead; (f) explosion; (g) fire; (h) flood; (i) earthquake; (j) tornado; (k) hurricane; (l) live, downed electrical wires; and (m) gas leak.

Death

Death includes the death of a classmate, student, teacher, parent, family member, employee, or prominent figure. Death might occur as a result of (a) natural death due to illness, (b) accidental death, (c) homicide, and (d) suicide. An individuals's death can have long-term devastating effects on other students, parents, teachers, administrators, and service providers.

RELATIONSHIP BETWEEN CRISES AND SPECIAL EDUCATION

There appears to be a mutually inclusive relationship between crisis situations and special education because of the attention given to persons who encounter disruption, disaster, and death-related incidents. Students experiencing crises cannot be reached by traditional educational programs–their programs must be modified and adapted to help them maximize their full potential. These students are usually atypical in nature; that is, they do not generally fit the stereotypical student mold. Logically, this makes them exceptional learners who need supplementary and additional education different from what is normally expected in the regular classroom. The adaptation and modification of programs usually become key operational variables for students who encounter out-of-the-norm experiences. More than a decade ago, Berdine and Blackhurst (1985) concluded that exceptional children are "children who have physical, mental, behavioral or sensory characteristics that differ from the majority of children such that they require special education and related services to develop to their maximum capacity" (p. 7). This generic definition also describes, to a very large extent, students experiencing crises.

In this text, we argue that students with exceptionalities and students in crises are atypical students who require multidimensional intervention strategies. The promulgation of the 1975 Education of All Handicapped Children Act (Public Law 94-142) and its reauthorization in 1990 as the Individuals with Disabilities Education Act (IDEA, Public Law 101-476) created a total mobilization stage for atypical students. To meet the unique needs of each student, the processes of identification, assessment, placement, and instruction in the least restrictive environment include provisions for parental consent, procedural safeguards, confidentiality of information, and the development of individualized education plans (IEPs; Hallahan & Kauffman, 1997; Heward, 1996). Based on the individualization embedded in special education, the uniqueness of each person and the effect of each crisis situation call for rethinking traditional crisis-intervention strategies and professional-preparation programs.

In some cases, a disruptive situation can be caused by disaster or death. In others, disaster can lead to disruption or death. Or death can have disruptive effects on students, teachers, and families. For instance, the death of a pet can have far-reaching disruptive effects on a student's concentration, attention span, and academic performance. This situation, as simple as it seems, can be problematic to a poorly prepared general or special educator who is quick to prejudge or label his or her student. In most cases, the birth of a child with a disability can be disruptive to siblings and parents. It has been well-documented that the presence of such a child creates parental shock, denial, frustration, anger, and depression (Gargiulo, 1985; Kroth, 1985; Simpson, 1996). When improperly managed, the birth of a child with a disability may lead to divorce, which can also have traumatic effects on children's coping and learning skills. In a related situation, the presence of a student with physical or health impairments can be disruptive, not only to the student, teacher, and parents, but also to classmates and their parents. Another example is the presence of a classmate with Acquired Immune Deficiency Syndrome (AIDS) such as the case of Ryan White which, a few years back, attracted national and world-wide attention as he struggled to do what other children and youth did—attend school. When he died, he became an inspirational symbol for those with the disease and those fighting hard to eradicate it.

Many school children come from drug-infested environments and are, thus, exposed to drug-related violence. Logically, violence affects their ability to concentrate and learn in school (Staff, 1996). These students are frequently at risk for misidentification, misassessment, miscategorization, misplacement, and even misinstruction (Obiakor, 1994; Obiakor & Algozzine, 1995). The challenge for general and special educators is to know if these students have learning problems or learning disabilities, behavior problems or behavior disorders, and cognitive readiness problems or mental disabilities.

NO ONE-MODEL INTERVENTION TECHNIQUE

About two decades ago, Sheehy (1976) remarked that "the courage to take new steps allows us to let go of each stage with its satisfactions and to find the fresh responses that will release the richness of the next. The power to animate all of life's seasons is a power that resides within us" (p. 514). Sheehy's statement buttresses the fact that human beings pass through different stages or situations, some of them caused by and some in reaction to crises. Invariably, there is a richness and satisfaction in tackling each crisis with zeal and power. Her statement summarizes an important idea of this book, namely that crises are a part of life. And because they are, the myriad of life crises like the life stages with which they are intertwined demand multidimensional crisis-intervention techniques.

The categories of life crises discussed in this book make it easier for parents and professionals to specifically address intervention strategies. When disruption, disaster, or death occurs, it may be unproductive to create unnecessary dichotomies during intervention. The reason is simple. One crisis can have a ripple effect on other crises. When this happens, a one-model intervention technique will fail. We propose throughout this book that collaborative efforts are needed in the identification, assessment, and intervention of crisis situations from prekindergarten to university levels. In the monograph, *Teacher Education for the Twenty-First Century* which resulted from the American Association of State Colleges and Universities (AASCU) conference held in June 1992, the association affirmed its vision of the "New American School" when it wrote

> It is probable that one school model will not suffice, but common threads will exist throughout the various models. The schools will be community based and will involve business, industry, social service agencies, government, parents, teachers, students, colleges, universities, and private advocacy groups. Collaboration will be essential. Many of the groups now viewed as external to the educational system will be involved in curriculum development and various school structures integral to change. Certainly, professionals from pre K-12 and higher education will be required to be involved fully in each others' systems. (p. 3)

This AASCU vision foreshadows partnership or teamwork in managing crises, resolving conflicts, solving problems, and preparing general and special education professionals to work with atypical students. A logical extension is that the effects and aftereffects of disruption, disaster, and death can be managed whether they appear individually or collectively. General and special educators must make good decisions as they incorporate techniques and personnel into their crisis intervention strategies. As the AASCU (1992) points out:

Along with making it possible for teachers to assume a greater role in administrative decision-making, New American Teachers will be encouraged to rediscover the call that originally summoned them to the teaching profession. Teachers always enter the classroom firmly committed to the principles that all children can learn, that each child is a valuable member of society, and that the young thrive in an atmosphere of caring. Caring teachers create an environment which intentionally summons students to realize their potential in all areas of human endeavor. Such an environment will generate trust among students, and parents will view education as a cooperative, collaborative activity where process is as important as product. (p. 6)

PERSPECTIVES

Disruption, disaster, and death are of great concern to all students, parents, general and special educators, and other service providers. Today, educators face a broader range of these situations daily. Even though crises might be viewed or handled differently from school to school or from community to community, students and their teachers consistently have difficulties dealing with them. It behooves schools to minimize the at-risk nature of these difficulties to the greatest possible extent. Instead of the "rat-race" for educational reforms that has led to illusionary results and conclusions, "real" solutions are needed to address "real" human problems of students. The inescapable issues of equity and inclusion, especially with regard to students in crises, must be emphasized. Traditional problems can no longer be tackled using traditional techniques. It is time to realize that life's problems can be overwhelming and that society can no longer afford to allow students to fall into the mode of learned helplessness.

In other words, general and special educators must utilize nontraditional identification, assessment, and instructional strategies to ameliorate multidimensional problems confronting students in crises. These students cannot be categorized or labeled; however, educators can make them realize that disruption, disaster, and death are crises that can be intervened and managed. General and special educators, service providers, and parents must understand the goals of helping with real life problems as discussed in this text. In the words of Holmes (1994):

The goal of helping with a real-life problem is effective maintenance, not cure. Psychological maintenance is directly equivalent to treating a chronic medical condition such as diabetes. Diabetes is not curable, but the patient can lead an otherwise healthy, productive, long life if proper medical attention is obtained and the treatment regimen is followed. Without denying the impact of the precipitating or ongoing event, the person with a real-life problem can learn to assimilate the emotional pain into his or her overall lifestyle. (p. 45)

DISCUSSION QUESTIONS

1. Briefly discuss the relationship among disruption, disaster, and death.

2. The authors indicated that school staff members and administrators need to be prepared for dealing with crisis situations. How well prepared is your school?

3. Imagine that a student in your class has a life-threatening disease (e.g., AIDS) which is causing some disruptive effects on your students and their parents. Briefly discuss your role as a crisis intervener in this critical situation.

4. This chapter states that no one model is appropriate for managing crisis situations. In your opinion, analyze the appropriateness of this statement as it relates to your school.

5. Briefly summarize how you managed a crisis situation in your classroom, home, or community.

CHAPTER 2

DISRUPTION

In a Louis Harris poll of teenagers (Harris, 1996), 36% said they feel safe around their school only sometimes, and 4% said they never feel safe. Schools are therefore no longer a haven where all students continually feel secure. Many events causing crises and disruptions can occur at any moment among students and school staff. As indicated in Chapter 1, a crisis is an unanticipated event that has a disruptive effect on a significant segment of the school population. It is unlimited in scope and frequently involves serious injury or even death. The serious injury may be emotional or psychological, not just physical. As Mehring (1995) states, "a disruption is an unauthorized event that significantly impacts the normal daily school routine or the population of the school" (p. 139). In this chapter, it is discussed in terms of its effects within any school setting.

NONVIOLENT DISRUPTION

There are many types of disruptions, some of which are discussed in this subsection. *Protesting* is a free speech issue. Peaceful protests, walkouts, and unauthorized assemblies can be considered examples. Some become more disruptive than others, but in any particular school, any one can be disruptive. For example, let us assume that the principal of a high school stopped the publication of the students' newspaper because it contained profane words. This meaningful action could lead to unpredictable disruptive protests from students and sympathetic teachers. School administrators might find these protests inappropriate and respond by suspending student protest leaders and firing the sympathetic teachers. Or students and sympathetic teachers might seek legal redress under the rubric of infringement of personal freedom. The media might even get involved because of the possible ramifications of infringement of the press, free speech, or other freedoms guaranteed by the Bill of Rights but subject to interpretation especially when being applied to individuals who are not yet legally adults or to a school situation.

Unlawful assembly of students or other personnel can have a disrupting influence. In numerous school districts throughout the country, requests are made to assemble in the school building for prayer. When organized, this activity is illegal within school buildings but can take place around the flagpole on school grounds. When the unlawful assembly occurs, some groups may protest the use of taxpayer money to pay for religion. If the group that advocates for prayer is not allowed to assemble, its sympathizers may protest the lack of respect for religion. In either case, disruption occurs.

Unmarried and/or teenage mothers populate many schools today. Approximately one million teenage girls become pregnant each year, which at the very least causes some disruption in their own lives. The responsibility of rearing babies and children can detract from academics and studying and leads to a high risk of dropping out for both the father and the mother (Muccigrosso, Scavarda, Simpson-Brown, & Thalacker, 1991). These students in essence lose their adolescence and the activities that go along with it. Many are forced to work in low paying and/or odd jobs to support and provide for their children. The burden created by these stressors can be disruptive to their present and future lives. Schools have continually struggled to provide students appropriate and relevant pregnancy-prevention programs and/or parenting education. The provision of appropriate social skills and independent living skills becomes a real challenge for general and special educators.

Children of divorce experience a crisis that sometimes spills over into the school. One in two U.S. marriages ends in divorce, and each year over a million children are involved in divorce proceedings. Today's typical family is a single-parent, blended, or step-family, not a nuclear family as in the past (King & Goldman, 1988). The classroom sometimes is the safest place for some children to act out their emotional feelings. For example, Abu's parents divorced 9 months ago. He seemed to have adjusted until he failed a test. He became so upset that he threw his chair across the room and knocked over his table. Some events, like Abu's test results, precipitate aggression, which in turn leads to disruption.

Cult invasion creates another disruption. Children who are alienated from their families and have low self-esteem are particularly prone to cult participation. The cults prey on the child's fears and may include such activities as rituals and devil worship. Cults affect students' school performance and participation, as well as community harmony. For instance, the Waco, Texas, incident with David Koresh and his followers (the Branch Davidians) disrupted the lives of many because of devastating incidents of gunshot, fire, and death. The investigation by the U.S. Congress revealed massive cases of child and sexual abuses, false assumptions of mystical powers, misjudgments by some law enforcement officers (e.g., the Alcohol, Tobacco, and Firearms agents of the U.S. Treasury Department), and deaths of law enforcement officers and Branch Davidians. Cult invasion may be a minor disruption on family and school lives, or it may have far-reaching, violent results.

VIOLENT DISRUPTION

Riots, such as those in Los Angeles in May 1993, can severely affect the operation of a school. When rioting begins near a school, there is always a concern for the welfare of students. Some critical questions deserve attention. Should the school dismiss and possibly endanger students either on their way home or by going to see what is transpiring? Is there a way to provide safe exit for students? What if the rioting gets close to the school? Because riots can last many hours, what happens to students if riots last longer than school time? The looting that often accompanies rioting also has serious ramifications to the community. And when a school reopens after a riot, it has to deal with student fears and concerns. For example, many students in inner city Los Angeles in 1993 knew people who were seriously injured and who had lost property.

Occasionally, a student is *kidnapped*. Often times, the kidnapper is a relative, usually a parent, who was not granted custody of the child or children. Not long ago, a mother of two young children was granted sole custody of her children and moved from Michigan to Kansas to get away from an abusive husband. For weeks, she drove these children to and from school until she finally relented and let them ride the school bus. Shortly thereafter, as her children got off the bus, two people—one of whom was their father—grabbed them and drove off in a car. Imagine the horror the other children felt as they saw their classmates whisked away screaming. The two children directly involved in the incident were eventually sent back to Kansas by a Michigan court order and returned to the school from which they had been kidnapped. Not only was their mother worried and overprotective of them but other parents were also worried and overprotective of their own children. The school district decided to design measures to prevent the repetition of such an incident in an effort to allay parents' fears.

In the same vein, *hostage situations* can be deadly with long-lasting effects. Also, for many years, *bomb threats* have disrupted schools. Sometimes students call in bomb threats as a prank or to get out of tests but threats also increase when a bombing has occurred. Pitcher and Poland (1993) mention a study indicating one school in a hundred reports a bomb threat each month. This can be very scary.

Child abuse can certainly be a disruptive influence. Physical or emotional abuse cuts across socioeconomic and ethnic backgrounds and happens all too frequently. Almost daily it seems, the popular media report children being severely injured or killed. Others are sexually abused, and although more sexual abuse happens to females, it also happens to boys. Between one-fourth and one-third of Americans experienced, as children, unwanted sexual advances from an adult (Pitcher & Poland, 1993). Abuse can lead to poor impulse control, poor attention span, poor grades, violence, and physical aggression. For instance, Sonia was a good student. After her mother remarried, Sonia's grades began to fall, and she became argumentative and involved in numerous fights. It was later determined she had been sexually abused by her stepfather and was beaten almost weekly.

Gang-related activities disrupt school whether they occur on school grounds or away from school property. In neighborhoods controlled by gangs, children still have to walk to school and may be accosted for money, hassled to purchase drugs, or threatened with physical violence. Affected students may come to school agitated and have difficulty learning. Harris (1996) indicated that the great majority (about 78%) of teens believe "gangs are violent and destructive" (p. 99). Initiation rights of gangs may include violence within the school. Initiates may be required to assault other youth, steal, sell drugs, or even rape. All of these activities are extremely disruptive and can lead to disaster and death.

Violent acts are occurring in schools with more frequency. Long (1992) reported that in one year alone property was stolen from 2.4 million students and 400,000 students were assaulted. A 1991 Bureau of Justice report indicated more than 400,000 students were victims of violent crimes at school between June 1988 and January 1989 (National School Safety Center, 1993). A major disruption in schools today relates to *weapons* which is why one can only enter some schools by going through a metal detector. Pitcher and Poland (1993) report that each year 70,000 weapon-related assaults take place in schools. According to Pitcher and Poland, 33% of students carry weapons of some kind to school. Hughes, Clarke, DeHotman, and Bean (1996) estimate that 135,000 students carry guns to school each day. Other items, daily used as weapons in schools, include pen guns, pen knives, belts, and brass knuckles. Hughes et al. also report that students bring weapons (a) to impress friends, (b) for self-esteem or to feel important, and (c) for self-defense. Because children take guns to school every day of the year, guns are a major source of school disruption.

Alcohol consumption occurs in children as young as five and one can readily find children of 9 or 10 using marijuana or alcohol. In a study of 9- to 12-year-olds, one-half of the students had experienced peer pressure to try drugs and alcohol (Pitcher & Poland, 1993). Approximately 57% of all high school students have used illicit drugs at least once. Today, crack cocaine is fast consuming students as it is a cheap, highly addictive drug. As Harris (1996) notes, teens indicated it is easy to get illegal drugs in their neighborhoods.

Drug dealing and selling on school grounds and within the buildings is a big business. Cellular phones make it convenient for students to arrange drug deals. General and special educators need to watch for strangers and older students hanging around school buildings as these could be drug pushers. Today, kids sell drugs to kids within schools, and students know who to see if they want drugs. Not long ago, a second grade teacher in Wisconsin found two students had overdosed in class. Investigators discovered a classmate's father was providing the drugs.

Other crises, related to *behavior problems and physical aggression*, occur in the school setting (Van Acker, 1996). These include cursing, grabbing one another, punching, slapping, teasing, threatening, harassing, intimidating, and bullying—and all detract from the learning environment. Usually, the perpetrator picks on a student who is more vulnerable and less able to defend against the attack or to fight back. Harris (1996) found a strong consensus among teenagers that peer pressure is to blame at least somewhat for violence against teens. Following are his startling polling results of teen activities (and the percentage of participation) based in some measure on peer pressure:

- Drinking alcoholic beverages (42%).
- Using drugs like marijuana, cocaine, or crack (38%).
- Becoming a member of a gang (37%).
- Holding drugs for someone (31%).
- Selling drugs (29%).
- Carrying a gun outside of home (24%). (p. 19)

Teenagers are likely to change their own behaviors as the result of a crime or the threat of one. Harris (1996) reported that nearly one-half of all teens have made at least one change in a daily routine because of a concern about crime or because of the threat of a crime. Changes include (a) switching to a different group of friends; (b) avoiding particular places, activities, or sports; (c) carrying a weapon; (d) altering the route to or from school; (e) skipping school or cutting classes; (f) performing more poorly in school; and (g) obtaining protection from peers.

Aggressive acts are not limited to students. *Emotionally out of control* staff members also disrupt schools. For example, Ms. Thomas had taught seventh grade English for 15 years and was considered a good teacher. However, early this year she was in the process of a divorce, her mother died, and her son was convicted of breaking and entering. This year's class had been poorly behaved and aggressive. One of her students, Mark, had severe behavior problems. When Ms. Thomas told him to return to his seat and go to work, he swore at her and refused to sit down. Ms. Thomas began screaming and hit him across the face. She became emotionally out of control and disrupted the school process.

Medical emergencies are sudden, unexpected occurrences that require immediate medical attention (Mehring, 1995). Such emergencies disrupt class and nearly always disrupt an entire school. The health and welfare of the involved person(s) is of utmost importance, especially if the condition is life threatening. In addition, *unexpected deaths* frequently cause disruptions. These may include the death of a student, employee, or prominent figure due to natural causes, illness, accidents, homicide, or suicide. See Chapter 4 for further discussions on death.

IMPACT OF DISRUPTION ON STUDENTS WITH EXCEPTIONALITIES

Students with exceptionalities are more susceptible to the ravishing effects of disruption because of the characteristics of their particular disabilities and because of their generally lower self-esteem. For example, they may resort to *carrying weapons* to get peers to be friends and to have a false sense of elevated self-esteem. Or they may *join a cult or gang* to feel a part of a group and thus raise their self-esteem.

Individuals with developmental disabilities are four times as likely to be *sexually abused* as individuals without disabilities (Muccigrosso et al., 1991). Data documenting the incidence and complexity of *teenage pregnancy and parenting* of students with exceptionalities is sparse, but problems confronting these students are sometimes greater than those of their nondisabled peers (Muccigrosso et al., 1991). They are more vulnerable because of their learning and/or emotional problems (i.e., lower intelligence, poor social skills, poor communication skills, poor decision-making skills, and lower self-esteem). Kleinfeld and Young (1989) note that a higher percentage of students with disabilities become pregnant and at an earlier age than teenagers who do not have disabilities.

The *use and abuse of alcohol and drugs* by students with exceptionalities are comparable with those of individuals without exceptionalities. However, individuals with emotional and behavioral disorders, learning disabilities, hyperactivity, or attention deficit disorders are more likely to exhibit characteristics overlapping those of substance-abusing students. Thus, they are more likely to abuse alcohol and drugs. Unfortunately, few studies on alcohol and drug abuse have been conducted on students with mental retardation, sensory disabilities, or physical disabilities (Leone, 1991).

Some researchers hypothesize that *aggression and violence* are increasing among students with special needs (Simpson, Miles, Walker, Ormsbee, & Downing, 1991). Also, students with serious emotional and behavioral disabilities are in general education school settings. As restrictive treatments and educational options decrease, these students become the responsibility of general education without an increase in resources. As a result, more aggression and violence will occur in schools.

The double jeopardy that occurs when students with exceptionalities find themselves in crisis situations calls for innovative intervention strategies (Webb, 1991). Unidimensional techniques will not work. We prescribe a Comprehensive Support Model (Obiakor, 1994) because remedies will be fruitless unless the self, the home, the school, and the community are connected. To help an exceptional student in crisis within a school, collaborative efforts of the regular educator, special educator, counselor, psychologist, therapist, and paraprofessional must be maintained.

INTERVENTION STRATEGIES FOR DISRUPTION

Every school should design its own plan of action for dealing with disruptions. One such plan has been the Crisis Intervention Team (CIT). CITs have been formed at many elementary and secondary schools to deal with events surrounding any unusual circumstances affecting faculty, staff, and/or students. These events might include those that demand immediate action (e.g., hostage situation, sniper on campus, suicide on campus, or evacuation of a building due to a gas leak) and those that are serious but not requiring immediate attention (e.g., untimely death of a student or staff member due to an accident, suicide, or illness).

According to Schoenfeldt and Associates (1994), the design of an effective crisis-response model for schools should include (a) a district emergency plan, (b) a crisis team at each site, and (c) a crisis plan for each school site. Expertise and support should be provided within the existing school community with professional assistance and guidance available as back-up. Intervention approaches involving outsiders "landing," taking over, and then departing soon after the crisis is over—so called "helicopter or paratrooper syndrome" approaches– should be avoided.

District Management Plan

An overall management plan should be designed and coordinated by a district-level CIT. Administrators and other individuals with special responsibility and/or expertise in crisis response (e.g., mental health professionals, police officials, and health professionals) should establish district-wide guidelines for crisis management, provide opportunities for district staff to receive adequate and ongoing training, ensure that each school has a fully operational crisis team, and coordinate special assignments of school and community personnel in the event of a crisis. School districts should develop a crisis plan *prior* to a crisis situation. Figures 2.1 and 2.2 present innovative crisis-intervention plans. Staff development activities within individual school buildings should be used to inform all staff members about the crisis plan. Specific plans of action may vary depending upon the crisis. In the event of a crisis, staff members should be knowledgeable about the sequence of events to be implemented and should be conscious of the appropriate communications to provide to students, the media, and interested community members.

Crisis Team

Teachers, counselors, administrators, secretaries, students, and/or support staff can volunteer to be members of the school-site CIT. Individuals can serve for one year or longer. A rule of thumb for crisis-team size is 2 members per 100 students. Team members serve three critical roles related to crisis situations: prevention, intervention, and postvention (Kadel & Follman, 1993; Mehring, 1995). The prevention role involves training in crisis-team functions, general first aid, risk assessment, and communication strategies. Intervention involves (a) site management in the event of a crisis; (b) communication with staff, students, parents, the community, and community agencies including fire, police, mental health, and hospitals; and (c) debriefing activities for staff, students, and parents. The addition and training of new members and participation in advanced training activities comprise the focus for postvention. CITs can be responsible for not only developing and implementing a crisis-management plan but also for recommending strategies for a safer school environment. Following are general principles for managing crises and building self-concepts (Mehring, 1995; Obiakor & Algozzine, 1995; Webb-Johnson, Obiakor, & Algozzine, 1995):

1. Intervene immediately—be proactive not reactive.
2. Target the intervention toward the precipitating situation; that is, be situation specific.
3. Provide correct information about the situation.
4. Give truthful and realistic assurance.
5. Empower the individual affected by the crisis by getting him or her involved in the intervention process.
6. Provide necessary emotional support without patronizing the individual.
7. Focus on accurate self-concepts (self-understanding, self-love, and self-empowerment).

Crisis Plan

In anticipation of a crisis event, the CIT should identify all necessary tasks for handling the incident and assign staff members for each task. Tasks might include (a) informing the district office; (b) accompanying injured students and/or staff to hospitals; (c) maintaining order and calm on campus; (d) coordinating transportation; (e) coordinating communication among the school, parents, and the media; (f) identifying students and adults who were injured or killed; and (g) notifying parents and spouses. The principal generally assumes authority in a crisis situation. Someone should be designated to fill this role in the event the principal is away from the building or incapacitated by the crisis event. A list of crisis-management procedures and the names of those responsible for various tasks should be posted in the school office, given to all staff, and maintained in the district office.

Once a crisis plan is developed, school staff should participate in training in crisis-intervention procedures and learn their responsibilities. Students should also receive crisis-management training and should have opportunities to practice emergency procedures. All school personnel need to be prepared to deal with a crisis situation. There will be occasions when administrators, counselors, and psychologists cannot provide immediate assistance to all who need it. General and special education teachers can be valuable in crisis intervention by providing immediate assistance to restore normality and to minimize lasting debilitating effects. They should

1. Announce events to students *after* facts are obtained through appropriate channels. Announcements should be factual and presented in a calm manner using age-appropriate terminologies. Unnecessary or confusing details should be avoided.

2. Lead class discussions about the event–discussions should focus on *feelings*, not opinions.

3. Identify students in need of counseling. It is necessary to be alert for those students whose reactions are more extreme than the norm and refer them to an appropriate counselor or resource person.

4. Generate activities to reduce the impact of trauma. Students should be given permission to express feelings. It is important to help students understand that they may be flooded with waves of emotion and that there is more than one way to deal with feelings.

5. Structure and shorten assignments.

6. Postpone testing.

Once an intervention plan for disruption has been developed, all members of each school staff within a district need to receive training that provides an overview of the plan and prepares each individual to fulfill a designated role should a disruptive crisis occur. Off-campus resources like police and fire departments and mental health agencies also need to be informed about the plan and their potential involvement.

A specific mechanism should be designed at the building and district level that will facilitate an immediate meeting of all necessary CIT members should the need arise. Many districts with crisis-intervention plans have specified phone trees to fulfill this purpose. In addition, key administrative personnel wear beepers and frequently have car phones.

Parents should also be apprised of how potential crisis situations are handled within the building and/or district. School procedures for dealing with a crisis or emergency situation can be published in student and/or parent handbooks. Reminders can be printed in school newsletters. Inservice sessions can be presented at meetings parents attend (e.g., Parent Teacher Organization meetings and Back to School Night).

Figure 2.1
CRISIS INTERVENTION PROCEDURES

1. Building administrator/crisis team leader verifies the event through preliminary source, parent contact, or police. Calls 911 if necessary. Prepares formal written statement.

2. Administrator/leader notifies the Superintendent and provides the formal written statement.

3. Administrator/leader phones team members. Activates calling tree for certified and classified staff. Distributes the formal written statement.

4. Administrator/leader activate crisis center(s) (office of counselor, nurse and/or administrator; gym; cafeteria).

5. Administrator/leader convenes crisis team to plan response (administrator, support personnel [counselor, psychologist, nurse], teacher and secretary).

6. Administrator/leader determines the need for district crisis team and assigns team members the duty of contacting them. Sets time and agenda for faculty meeting.

7. Designated team member(s) announce the event to students and the time for a faculty meeting.

8. Crisis team members carry out assignments in the areas of logistics, students, staff, parents, media, and victim's family.

9. Crisis team assesses the need for additional support and follow-up activities.

10. Team holds a crisis debriefing.

Figure 2.2
CRISIS INTERVENTION PLAN FOR AN INTRUDER

The intruder can be a gunman, kidnapper, thief, or any violent person. Steps to take include

1. Summon emergency help–call 911 if necessary.

2. Take whatever action is appropriate to reduce danger to students and staff such as

    • Isolate the intruder.

    • Evacuate the building.

    • Move students to another location within the building.

    • Stay in classrooms with doors closed and/or locked.

3. If the intruder is outside the building, move students inside and lock outside doors.

4. Notify central office.

After the intruder is apprehended by police

5. Decide if students should be taken to an alternate location.

6. Decide if students should return to class or be dismissed early.

7. Maintain student roster for dismissal.

8. Write a press release.

9. Determine need for follow-up support to those involved and their families.

Intervention plans for disruptions should undergo periodic review. Petersen and Straub (1992) propose a review whenever major changes occur in a school such as "an increase in attendance; the addition of portable or new structures; multihandicapped programs; or an increase in team travel" (p. 11). The importance of a crisis-intervention plan cannot be overstated. The plan, however, is only as good as those responsible for carrying it out. Every staff member must be briefed and rebriefed. Phone numbers must be updated, blueprints of all facilities must be in place, and materials and equipments must be in working order if the plan is to be successful. According to Leviton and Greenstone (1989), the five major components of effective crisis intervention are

1. *Immediacy*: A CIT member must attempt to relieve anxiety, prevent disorientation, and ensure that additional harm does not occur. Immediacy requires quick and effective action.

2. *Control*: Because those closest to the crisis may be out of control, the intervener or CIT member must ensure control of the situation. Sometimes control is gained passively, simply through the visibility of an intervener or CIT. Other situations will require firm and direct supervision and instructions to key school personnel, students, and perhaps, family members. The goal of control is to protect those involved—victims, the intervener, CIT members, bystanders, and significant others—and to diffuse the emotionality present in almost all crisis situations.

3. *Assessment*: A quick, accurate, and comprehensive evaluation of the precipitating events and crisis situations must be conducted. The assessment must be conducted in a calm and reassuring manner. The intervener or CIT member must be willing to reach out to victims both emotionally and physically as needed.

4. *Disposition*: Those involved must be assisted to effectively manage the crisis situation. Resources are mobilized to assist those involved to bring a sense of control and structure to the situation.

5. *Referral/Follow-Up*: Ongoing assistance must be provided. Once the immediate crisis is under control, victims may need ongoing support to assist them to effectively manage the resulting feelings and reac-

tions to the crisis situation. Individuals may require referral to social service agencies and/or professional resources.

To effectively manage disruptions and reduce crises affecting students in schools, other intervention strategies must be adopted and implemented. These important strategies are discussed next.

Establish Strategic Communication. To enhance security, strategic communication should be developed. For instance, code phrases or slang terms should be established and announced over the school intercom to signal teachers and students of emergency situations. Teachers in portable units and those providing instruction outside the building should be notified personally if emergency precautions and/or actions are necessary. Faculty, staff, and students should be provided clear instructions regarding appropriate actions until the crisis is over. Regular updates on events facilitate calmness and dispel rumors. Teachers are generally the most direct link to students. Therefore, they should be kept informed through faculty meetings and/or memos explaining what has happened and what constitutes the school or district response.

Parents must be informed whenever a crisis event affects a school. If only one or a few students are involved (e.g., explosion in chemistry class or student suicide), personal contact with parents of the affected students is mandatory. If, on the other hand, the entire school of 1,500 students is affected, other means of parent notification must be sought. In a noninjury situation like a broken gas main or power outage, students could be provided with a note to parents explaining events. Many schools have classroom calling trees for parents, listing both home and work phones. Depending upon the severity of the situation, public media like the radio and television could be contacted to assist with not only parent communication but also informed communication with the community.

Once information about a serious crisis situation is made public, many individuals including parents, concerned citizens, and the media will likely seek additional information. A school district or building employee should be responsible for responding to such inquiries. If more than one person will be asked to respond, a prepared statement should be used by all individuals to ensure consistency in the information provided.

Once the crisis situation has been alleviated, administrators, faculty, staff, students, and the CIT members should participate in debriefing activities. The first 3 days after a crisis, the team should (a) provide time for students and staff to search for meaning in the crisis event, (b) engage individuals in understanding and accepting personal reactions, (c) increase the school community's ability to cope with future adversities, and (d) refine the crisis-intervention plan. Depending upon the severity of the crisis, ongoing individual or group counseling may be needed by some of the individuals involved directly or indirectly in the crisis.

Adopt the National Education Service Foundation Plan. The National Education Service Foundation (1994) developed a 12-point plan to curb the rise of violence among the nation's youth. Each point should be reviewed by local school districts in an effort to develop proactive rather than reactive plans for effectively anticipating and managing potential contributors to violence and possible disruption to the learning process. These points are

1. Provide prenatal and early childhood programs for at-risk populations.

2. Expand parent education and family support programs.

3. Provide violence prevention programs (e.g., teaching peer helping and nonviolent models of conflict resolution).

4. Provide and integrate family support services that affect children including schools, day care, and health care.

5. Restrict everyone's access to instruments of aggression (e.g., by reforming the gun industry, requiring tighter restrictions on gun dealers, and enforcing stronger annual liabilities for illegal sales).

6. Reduce and reform the instances of violence purveyed to the public as entertainment, including movies, television, music, and video games.

7. Educate families about the risks of maintaining firearms in the home.

8. When appropriate, encourage the use of effective alternatives to incarceration for youth and the use of effective rehabilitation programs for violent youth who are incarcerated.

9. Expand the constellation of interventions based on health and pre-adolescent and adolescent development that includes having caring adults in the lives of young people.

10. Expand cutting-edge programs (which include outreach to young males) that help prevent teen pregnancy.

11. Enforce zero toleration for the possession of guns in schools.

12. Support programs that reduce violence in the family as a way to curb youth violence by making homes safer for mothers, children, and ultimately, all family members. (National Education Service Foundation, 1994, pp. 42-44)

Utilize Teen Health Centers. Teen Health Centers (THCs) are available in many communities throughout the country. They are often associated with Departments of Human Services, job training program agencies, mental health centers, women's health services, Young Men's Christian Associations (YMCAs), Young Women's Christian Associations (YWCAs), or other social service agencies. The THC is a resource designed to assist students in identifying problems that could interfere with a successful educational experience. A secondary goal of the THC is to provide access to community services through removing barriers such as transportation, scheduling problems, and cost. Students can access the THC to obtain information and to receive assistance with personal concerns such as adjustment problems, social concerns, nutritional problems, pregnancy, substance abuse, and health problems. Students may also be referred to appropriate community agencies for assistance. Access to the THC should be student initiated. Parents who do not wish their children to participate should be given the opportunity to have them excluded from using THC services.

Report Violent Incidents. Disruptions may involve violent incidents between students; students and teachers or staff members; parents and students; parents and teachers/staff members; or teachers/staff and teachers/staff. Rapp, Carrington, and Nicholson (1992) found that many schools, wishing to avoid bad publicity, possible legal action, or elevation of the situation to a more serious level, do not have a formal plan for reporting incidents. Kadel and Follman (1993) suggest that *every* school should require *every* violent incident to be reported: "Acknowledging crime and reporting it accurately are crucial to understanding the extent of the problem and what is required to address it" (p. 10). An effective incident report should describe how, why, when, and where the incident happened; who was involved; and what action if any was taken by school personnel in response to the situation.

Enhance Campus Safety. Kadel and Follman (1993) outline several strategies for reducing disruptions in schools including increased surveillance; implementation of a no-weapons policy; techniques for keeping unauthorized individuals off campus; and ideas for enlisting student, parent, and community support. To increase surveillance and supervision around the school, staff, students (if appropriate), or parent volunteers can be assigned to monitor critical areas (e.g., halls, locker rooms, restrooms, and school grounds) where disruptions might occur. Security officers can also be employed. To increase safety, a buddy system can be instituted for teachers and/or students who remain at school after hours. In some settings, police officers or metal detectors may need to be employed to enhance campus safety.

A no-weapons policy should clearly define what will be construed as a weapon, where weapons will be prohibited (in the school building and on school grounds including athletic fields or parking lots), and what the consequences are for possessing a weapon. Individuals can be discouraged from unauthorized access to schools through implementing the surveillance and supervision strategies previously described. In addition, visitors should be asked to sign in and out at the main office upon entry and exit and to wear an identification or visitor badge while in the building. Some schools designate only one entrance for visitors during the school day. Security personnel or parent volunteers are posted at all other entries to enforce the policy. Staff and student cars can be required to have school parking stickers. Illegally parked cars can easily be identified by parent volunteers, noting make, license plate number, and color. If an incident should occur on campus, this information will provide one avenue for follow-up. Students should be notified of policies and procedures for having guests (from out of town or another school) at school. The same code of conduct that applies to students attending the school should also apply to guests. In addition, visibility within and outside the school should be promoted through well-lit buildings and grounds, and observable lockers, playgrounds, stairwells, and entryways.

Student, parent, and community support for a safe school environment can be solicited through providing support for students who are at risk. Two support strategies—Care Teams and Student Assistance Teams—are described later. In addition, encouraging teachers and students to avoid wearing valuable jewelry or clothing may reduce the potential for violent disruptions. Developing procedures for reporting disruptive behaviors may also stem its occurrence. Some schools allow anonymous reporting, while others require the individual doing the reporting to be identified to school officials. Feature stories about safe school practices in local community newspapers or on radio or TV broadcasts can be used to inform the community about school policies and consequences for violation of these policies. Parents and influential community members can be informed about the school crisis-intervention plan and be enlisted to reinforce conflict-resolution strategies in the neighborhood and throughout the community. Safe School Week activities and the use of school facilities on evenings and weekends by community groups can increase involvement of community members in local school efforts. This, in turn, can lead to Adopt-a-School programs by local businesses, volunteer programs by businesses and industry, and general increased awareness of community schools.

Develop Staff Inservice. Teachers and staff frequently upgrade knowledge and skills through professional inservice sessions. Crisis intervention should be an area of staff development for all school personnel. The district and building crisis-intervention plan, staff responsibilities, safe school practices, and student codes of conduct are samples of topics that should be addressed through staff development. Every member of the school staff including teachers, bus drivers, cafeteria workers, secretaries, and custodians all need to be well informed and fully involved in the crisis-intervention process.

Create Nondisruptive/Nonviolent Alternatives. The development and implementation of a crisis intervention plan, the articulation of a student code of conduct, the creation of safe school practices, and the preparation of school staff members to deal with varied types of school disruption will all increase the likelihood that if a crisis occurs, effective and efficient management will ensue. One additional strategy is to teach students how and why to avoid conflict and/or resolve it peacefully. Students can be taught how to (a) avoid being a victim of crime or violence; (b) resolve conflict; (c) engage in personal safety; (d) balance dating and relationship expectations; (e) be knowledgeable about laws (especially those impacting drinking and use of drugs), gang activities, and alternatives; and (f) put in practice problem-solving skills including anger control, social skills, and gun awareness.

For some students, especially those who prove to be disruptive or aggressive or who engage in bullying behavior, character education may be as critical as, or more important than, the academic curriculum. Students identified as having behavior problems should have social skills and self-esteem building objectives regularly included in the IEP. Unidentified students who engage in disruptive behaviors should be taught how to resolve disputes, make good decisions, and work cooperatively with others. According to Gronsnickle and Stephens (1992), teachers can assist students to develop a sense of personal and social responsibility through lessons on accountability for one's actions, patience and delayed gratification, and consequence-guided decision making.

Goldstein, Harootunian, and Conoley (1994) recommend a "comprehensive programming" intervention approach. The comprehensive programming model urges multidimensional planning that is both rehabilitative and preventive. School (students, teachers, and other school personnel), home, community, and police resources should be combined to design programming which includes

1. An in-school gang prevention curriculum (should include training in problem solving and gang-resistance techniques and ways to enhance self-esteem and increase awareness of negative factors of gang membership).

2. A model dress code (students should be prohibited from wearing gang clothing and jewelry and from grooming behavior signifying gang membership).

3. Enhanced understanding of graffiti (read it, record it, and remove it).

4. A gang-reporting hotline (should be easy, practical, and safe for students to use).

5. Support and protection of victims of gang violence (should include debriefing, counseling, and use of school placement adjustments as safety needs warrant).

6. Inservice training of teachers and other school personnel (should address signifiers of gang membership, intervention and prevention alternatives, and available safety measures).

7. A visitor screening policy (involves the employment of security personnel, establishing identification requirements, maintaining a log book, posting signs in appropriate languages, and directing visitors to the school office).

8. Parent notification (involves informing parents of apparent gang involvement combined with parent training in skills useful in diverting their children away from gang membership).

9. Community networking (combining the efforts of parents, law enforcement, students, and school personnel in shared attempts to minimize and counteract gang inroads at school).

10. A vibrant extracurricular program (attractive, youth-oriented programming which provides alternatives to gang membership and builds self-esteem, a sense of identity, peer companionship, and excitement). (Goldstein et al., 1994, pp. 163-164)

Foster Interagency Collaboration. "Too often, the comprehensive needs of children and youth go unmet due to a lack of interagency collaboration, and the blame for failure gets passed from one agency to another" (Kadel & Follman, 1993, p. 40). Schools are in a unique position to establish collaborative relationships with other agencies including law enforcement; social service providers; early childhood specialists; mental health counselors; medical practitioners; court judges and probation officers; parks and recreation representatives; and state department officials from education, health, and human resources. Key contact persons can work with school personnel in the event of a district- or building-wide crisis or on behalf of an individual student.

Clarify and Publicize Student Code of Conduct. A student code of conduct should be an integral component of a comprehensive district or building program for anticipating and managing disruption. A code of conduct clarifies for the student what responsible behavior is or is not. It informs administrators, staff, and students of limits or consequences to be issued by the principal or designee to students who have chosen to commit infractions of the code.

Every district and school should develop, distribute (to parents, students and staff), and enforce a code of conduct. Many disruptions may violate the conduct code. Unless a serious act of violence involves criminal charges, most conduct code infractions engage school officials in determining consequences. A code of conduct spells out ahead of time what the rules are and which consequences will be employed should the code be violated (e.g., assault, violent crime, weapon possession, drug usage or possession, bigotry, hate crimes, sexual harassment, and sexual assault). All rules included within the code of conduct should be consistently and fairly enforced. Figure 2.3 is a sample conduct code detailing alcohol and drug policies for one Midwestern school district which has consistently used this code as an effective way to resolve disruptive conflicts and facilitate student learning. Alternatives such as mediation are used for infractions such as dress code violations, use of abusive language, and disruptive behaviors on the school bus. Options for dealing with serious disruptions or code infractions include

1. *In-School Suspension.* This consequence for a student's misbehavior removes the student from classroom and extracurricular activities for one or more days through assignment to an in-school suspension classroom, the counselor's office, Saturday school, or after-school detention. Many schools engage the student in academic tutoring and/or counseling in an effort to curb future incidents that may require more serious actions by the school. In fact, a key advantage to in-school suspension is the opportunity to provide rehabilitation (tutoring and/or counseling), and follow-up reinforcement for appropriate adherence to the school conduct code. To be successful, this option needs "clearly defined rules and procedures, monitoring, and

student help built in" (Kadel & Follman, 1993, p. 14). Disadvantages of an in-school suspension include increased staff time for supervision, tutoring, counseling, and space, that is, a classroom or office to "house" students assigned to in-school suspension.

2. *Out-of-School Suspension.* Any student who presents a danger to self or others may be removed from school for one or more days. The U.S. Department of Justice (1986) noted that out-of-school suspension "removes violent students from school, is easy to administer, requires little planning or resources, and can be applied for a number of infractions" (p. 12). A key concern with this practice is that it is rarely coupled with long-term preventive and/or rehabilitative strategies. Research investigations by Comerford and Jacobson (1987) and Wheelock (1986) did not validate out-of-school suspension as a means of decreasing disruptive behaviors. A second key concern is that while the student is out of school, he or she is often unsupervised, thereby opening the door for delinquent behaviors.

3. *Expulsion.* Generally, schools use expulsion as a last resort or as a consequence for the most serious and/or threatening incidents. Unless the district and/or community has an alternative program, expelled youth are permanently displaced into unsupervised situations with minimal opportunities for rehabilitation. Many expelled students get into trouble with the law. Silva (1992) found that disproportionately high numbers of minorities are expelled without adequate procedural safeguards.

4. *Service Assignments.* Service assignments are challenging and rewarding—they instill responsibility and create opportunities for success. The most successful service assignments provide a contribution to the school or community and earn genuine and positive recognition from peers. Students engage in supervised work before or after school, on weekends, or during elective classes. Examples of appropriate service activities include serving as hall monitors; working in the school office; removing graffiti; tutoring younger students; and helping with landscaping, painting, or restoration work on school grounds (Task Force on School Discipline, 1990).

Figure 2.3
SAMPLE ADMINISTRATIVE PROCEDURES FOR ENFORCEMENT OF THE ALCOHOL/DRUG POLICY

These procedures are to insure the consistent enforcement of the Shawnee Mission District Alcohol/Drug policy. The procedures are in effect on school property or at any school-sponsored or school-sanctioned event. These administrative procedures describe the step-by-step process which must be followed in each case involving: possession, use, or distribution of illegal drugs (to include alcohol as well as other illegal and/or harmful substances); the possession, use, or distribution of tobacco; the possession, non-prescription use, or distribution of steroids; improper use of legal substances (to include prescription drugs, over-the counter medications and other products); the distribution of any substance if that substance is purported to be a controlled substance; or the possession or distribution of paraphernalia. Improper use of prescription drugs is defined as:

> "the use by a person other than the person for whom the script was written, or in dosage other than the dosage prescribed."

Improper use of over-the-counter medications or other products is defined as:

> "the use in amounts greater than the recommended dosage on the label, or for purposes other than those stated on the label."

Drug Use/Under-The-Influence (Except Tobacco)

A. *First Offense*

Step 1:   If there is evidence of drug use or improper use of prescription drugs, over-the-counter medication or other products, or if a legitimate medical reason for the

Figure 2.3, *Continued*

behavior is not evident, the administrator detains the student under direct observation by an appropriate person.

Step 2: The administrator determines if medical help is needed. IF THERE IS ANY CONCERN ABOUT THE NEED FOR EMERGENCY MEDICAL HELP, THE APPROPRIATE ASSISTANCE SHOULD BE CALLED IMMEDIATELY. The school is *not* to transport.

Step 3: The administrator calls a parent or guardian, informing the parent or guardian of the nature of the problem, and requiring the removal of the student from the school setting.

Step 4: The administrator may call the police or security officer.

Step 5: A parent conference will be held.

Step 6: During the ensuing conference, the student and parent(s) or guardian(s) are to be informed that there is evidence that the student has been using or is/was under-the-influence of substances (named, if known,) and is immediately suspended for five days. A hearing before the District's Suspension and Expulsion committee will be scheduled if the administrator deems it appropriate. *These penalties are in addition to any legal obligations the student may have.*

Step 7: The following alternatives to Step #6, *exclusive of any legal obligation the student may have,* shall be offered to the

Continued on next page.

Figure 2.3, *Continued*

parent(s) or guardian(s) and student with all costs assumed by the student:

a.   Two day suspension, assessment by licensed alcohol and drug assessment or treatment agency, followed by the plan of care or treatment recommended by the assessing agency. The other three days are held, pending completion. It shall be the responsibility of the student and his/her parents to sign a release of information form, and to make sure that the agency sends the proper notification to the appropriate person in the school.

Recognizing that alcohol and other drug addiction is a disease, a student who accepts treatment will be treated as any student would be for any illness, regarding benefits and privileges as long as the student is making satisfactory progress in the program. (This statement does *not* supersede contracts signed by activity/athletic participants.)

b.   Two day suspension, assessment by licensed alcohol and drug assessment or treatment agency, participation of student in an 8-10 week, in-school intervention group *if the assessment deems it appropriate* (available only at schools with designated intervention counselors). The other three days are held, pending completion. It shall be the responsibility of the student and his/her parents to sign a release of information form, and to make sure that the agency and the Intervention Counselor send the proper notification to the appropriate person in the school.

5. *Alternative Schools/Schools Within Schools.* The National School Safety Center (1990) described alternative schools as a beneficial option for students with a history of disruptive and/or violent behaviors. Individualized learning, appropriate conduct, self-discipline, and personal responsibility are stressed. Employment apprenticeship programs are sometimes included as a component of this option.

To be implemented properly, a code of student conduct must not be used in any way that is perceived as unfair or biased; students and teachers must be treated with dignity. A code of conduct protects the rights of students who come to school to learn and articulates consequences for those who choose to violate the code by behaving irresponsibly or disrupting the learning environment.

Establish and Use Mediation. Mediation is a process whereby a neutral third party intervenes between two or more disputing parties to assist them in reaching a mutually accepted agreement. Mediation is offered as an alternative for resolving the conflict, and participation in the process should be voluntary. The goal of peer mediation is to empower students to develop life skills, such as listening and sensitivity awareness. The Kansas City, Missouri, School District (1993) listed five main objectives of peer mediation. They are

1. To promote harmony and understanding among students by providing peaceful means to resolve disputes and by teaching positive communication skills.
2. To improve the overall climate of the school.
3. To reduce the number of conflict situations that arise on school property and result in administrative conferences, student injury, or in-school or out-of-school suspensions.
4. To internalize the concepts of peacemaking.
5. To make more time for teaching. (p. 5)

Conflict Mediation/Conflict Resolution. Conflict mediation is particularly useful with children and youth who display antisocial behavior and alienation or rebelliousness. Students exhibiting antisocial behavior at an early age demand a great deal of time and energy from teachers. Quick interventions usually include rewards, threats, and isolation. These are often followed by suspension and referral for special education. None of these consequences equip students with the skills needed to become productive adults. Many consequences may result in increased antisocial behavior. Conflict mediation provides students with an understanding of the conflict, the ways a conflict escalates or diffuses, and strategies for cooperative problem solving.

Few students who feel alienated or rebellious respond to external motivational sources such as incentive programs, privilege removal, or threats. Conflict mediation promotes an internal locus of control, self-awareness, and an acceptance of differing points of view. Adolescents who fight, steal, or misbehave in school often have their freedom restricted by parents and/or teachers. This can be perceived by teenagers as threats to their need for independence, and power struggles often result. Conflict resolution promotes problem solving without severing crucial bonds needed during this developmental period. Problems can be "fixed" without threatening or restricting freedom. Conflict-mediation programs can be implemented in various forms. In general, most are based on the following assumptions (see O'Rourke, 1993):

1. Conflict is an unavoidable part of living and can be used as an opportunity for student learning and personal growth.

2. Because conflict is unavoidable, learning conflict-resolution skills is as educational and as essential to the long-term success of young people as learning geometry or history.

3. Students can resolve their conflicts with the assistance of other students as effectively as—if not more so than—they can with the assistance of adults.

4. Encouraging disputing students to collaboratively resolve the causes of present conflict is a more effective method of preventing future conflict (and developing student responsibility) than administering punishment for past actions.

O'Rourke (1993) indicates that conflict resolution teaches students to (a) deal with anger constructively, (b) communicate feelings and concerns without using violence and abusive language, (c) think critically about alternative solutions, and (d) agree to solutions in which all parties win. Conflict-resolution programs may differ in the number and combinations that mediators use. Teachers, students, and/or parents can be used as mediators. Following are several basic components of an effective conflict-resolution program:

1. Mediation is always voluntary—students must want to participate.

2. If drugs or weapons are involved, mediation is bypassed and a report is filed immediately with school authorities.

3. All parties at the mediation must adhere to the following ground rules:

   a. Each disputant speaks without interruption.

   b. Information shared during the conflict-resolution session is held in strict confidence.

   c. Mediators strive to create a conducive, neutral atmosphere.

   d. Mediators are committed to facilitating agreement, not manipulating or dictating the outcome.

   e. No shouting or name calling is allowed.

One of the positive outcomes of conflict resolution is that students take ownership of their own actions rather than responding to consequences imposed through contrived discipline plans. Second, students in conflict are actively involved in reaching consensus for solving the conflict in a nonviolent manner. Students are given the responsibility to control a potentially out-of-control situation. The third, and perhaps most important, outcome is that students acquire the procedures, skills, and attitudes needed to resolve conflicts constructively in their personal lives at home, in school, at work, and in the community. Interestingly, conflict resolution has been used successfully with preschoolers through high school seniors. This approach has been found to be a successful strategy for students with disabilities, especially those with behavior disorders (Mehring, 1995). An appropriate implementation of a conflict-resolution program requires 15 to 25 hours of training for those who intend to serve as mediators.

Peer Mediation. In peer mediation, students are trained to be peacemakers. Johnson and Johnson (1991) outline a plan for training students for the peer mediation role that entails "defining the conflict, exchanging positions and proposals, viewing the situation from all perspectives, inventing options for mental gain, and reaching a wise agreement" (p. 11). Peer mediators are taught to gain consensus from the parties involved in a conflict and to find a solution. Peer mediators provide ground rules to which all parties must agree. Students must solve the conflict without resorting to name calling. They must allow each other to speak without interruption and must be honest. In addition, to accomplish this peacemaker program, they must follow through on implementing an agreed-upon resolution and hold whatever is discussed in mediation sessions as confidential.

Ideally, all students in a class are trained in the negotiation and conflict-mediation steps. Two class members are selected to serve as peer mediators each day. Any conflict that students cannot resolve themselves is referred to designated peer mediators. The role of the peer mediator is rotated each day so all class members have an opportunity to serve. Peer mediation actively engages students in making decisions about issues and conflicts affecting their lives and addresses only part of the mediation challenge (i.e., student-student disputes). Its usefulness can be maximized in resolving disputes involving student-teacher, student-parent, parent-teacher, staff-staff, and staff-administrators.

Establish Care Teams. The 1990s may well be referred to as "the decade of the at-risk student" in the American educational system. Today, too many schools defer to others the responsibility of tackling many of the toughest problems facing American teenagers. To change this trend, schools can implement a systematic analysis of students who may be classified as "at risk." Chronic and acute symptoms of at risk students include, but are not limited to, the following:

1. Failure to demonstrate minimum competencies on statewide academic assessments.

2. Poverty.

3. Retention in one or more grades.

4. Fifteen or more absences during the previous year.

5. Suspension two or more times during the school year.

6. Adjudication as a juvenile offender.

7. Pregnancy or a parent.

8. Limited English proficiency.

9. Victim of physical, sexual, or emotional abuse.

10. Health and/or substance abuse problems.

11. Suicide attempt.

12. Academic deficiencies as evidenced by grade point average and/or test scores.

Care Teams are building-level teams that exist to support and recommend service for at-risk students. Individuals comprising the team should represent all areas of expertise within the building (e.g., administrators, teachers, school psychologists, social workers, counselors, school nurses, custodian and cafeteria personnel, parents, and/or students). Care Teams must meet on a regular basis, at least every 2 weeks. Student referrals should come to the team from a variety of sources, and the team is responsible for recommending a full range of interventions to decrease the at-risk nature of the student. Interventions may include in-building as well as district and community resources. To effectively deal with disruptions, the Care Team must engage in an ongoing follow-up of each active case until it is placed on an inactive list. All teachers and staff within a building must be engaged in staff development activities at the beginning of each school year to acquaint themselves with the Care Team mission, function, and referral procedures. Parents must also be informed about the Care Team. Care Team activities are often based on a set of underlying beliefs, namely,

1. It is a legitimate role of the school to intervene in situations which are inhibiting students' learning.

2. The staff can improve student learning through collaboration.

3. The school has an obligation to work with parents.

4. The team coordinates intervention services and strategies for dealing with disruptions.

5. The Care Team provides assistance not therapy.

6. The Care Team will not solve every problem or avert every crisis.

7. Confidentiality does not exist when a student is in danger.

8. The Care Team has an obligation to intervene in situations potentially dangerous to a student with or without the student's permission.

It is important for the Care Team to keep its activities consistent with the school's primary focus—student learning. When students have problems preventing them from learning, it is the responsibility of the Care Team to provide intervention strategies needed to maximize student learning. It is not the responsibility of the Care Team to personally provide all interventions; however, it is the charge of the team to identify available strategies and lead the school in developing programs to actualize student learning.

School-based resources might include the development of support groups, assemblies, and inservice sessions on varied topics including self-esteem, stepfamilies, substance abuse and recovery, new student adjustments, grief and loss, anger control, at risk for dropping out, social skills, and teen parenting. For students who are acting out, withdrawn, or experiencing family problems or a decline in academic performance, possible interventions might include meeting with the student or parent, referral to community resources (e.g., mental health), referral to a focus group within the school (e.g., eating disorders), referral for tutoring or mentoring, and discussion with specific teachers regarding effective study habits. To buttress the tasks of the Care Team, the following programs are needed:

1. Focus groups.

2. Individual counseling for students.

3. School programs such as Students Against Drunk Driving (SADD) and other antidrugs programs.

4. Wellness programs.

5. Gifted student tutor program.

6. New student orientation.

7. Teacher mentor program.

Establish Student Assistance Teams. Students can experience a number of problems that can have adverse effects on their school behavior, conduct, or academic performance. Such problems could lead to learning disabilities, physical illness, emotional and psychological problems, family or legal problems, and alcohol or other substance abuse. The school should become concerned when any of these problems repeatedly and definitely interfere with a student's school performance or jeopardize the health, safety, welfare, educational opportunity, or rights of other students or personnel.

Student Assistance Teams (SATs) are composed of teachers, secretaries, counselors, administrators, nurses, and coaches who volunteer to be members of the team. The purposes of the SAT are to

1. Provide assistance to students troubled by physical, emotional, social, legal, sexual, medical, family, or drug-use problems.

2. Improve the school's quality of education and the school environment.

3. Utilize existing human resources rather than require new professional staff.

4. Enlist the support and involvement of all professional staff members.

5. Focus on students' academic concerns which may be affected by major social problems.

The first objective of the SAT is to identify, as soon as possible, those students who are having problems. Early intervention can often help to resolve problems more easily. Students may voluntarily seek help or be identified by a staff member, parent, or friend. It is important that the nature and security of the problem be understood so appropriate help can be offered. Severe problems should be referred to appropriate community resources for professional assistance. Once a problem has been identified and the extent of the problem known, the student is encouraged to accept the services needed. SAT members help students consider possible options and encourage them to make decisions that will resolve problems in a positive way. The type of assistance provided will vary with the type and severity of the problem. It is *not* the function of the school or SAT to provide formal therapy. SATs provide support for students as they respond to assistance programs, make adjustments in lifestyles, and seek to make appropriate life decisions.

Within 24 hours of receiving a referral, SAT members seek information from all staff who have contact with the student. Once information is obtained, SAT members meet to discuss the referral and recommend a plan of action. The team decides whether the student should be referred to a school resource or to an outside agency. The team may also decide that more information is needed before a recommendation for action can be formulated. The team may choose to interview the parent(s) and/or student to obtain more information. It is recommended that two team members be present for student interviews. (Three or more members may be considered threatening, and one is not enough.) After a plan of action is formulated, the SAT meets with the parent and/or student and explains their recommendations. If a referral is made to an outside agency, release of information forms will require parent signature(s) or student signature if the student is of legal age. Parents and the student if within legal age do have the right to refuse to sign the release-of-information form.

The SAT should regularly devote a portion of scheduled meetings for reviewing the progress of referred students. A team member should be assigned to serve as case manager for each referred student and provide progress updates to team members. Specific information provided to the team should include (a) whether the SAT recommendation for action was carried out; (b) what progress the student is making; and (c) whether the case should be reexamined by the team, receive long-term monitoring, or be considered completed. It is important to note that no records of a student's involvement with the SAT must be kept in the cumulative folder. Any SAT records must be maintained separately from official school records. Participation in a SAT program should remain confidential and should be subject to state and federal regulations governing confidentiality and release of information.

Establish Teacher Assistance Teams. The purpose of Teacher Assistance Teams (TATs) is to support teachers and offer them a venue for consulting with fellow teachers regarding students with behavior, academic, and social concerns. At the elementary level, the TAT is ideally comprised of two primary and two intermediate teachers. These four teachers meet with the identified teacher and offer suggestions and recommendations for addressing the concern. Even in small high schools, a TAT of about two to four teachers can be imple–mented. Team members should represent varied disciplines (e.g., science and English). In larger high schools, several four-member TATs may be desirable. TATs provide moral and literal support for teachers so they understand they are not alone in difficult situations. The needs of teachers associated with implementing least restrictive environment settings should be included. The main concern associated with TATs is finding the time needed for meetings. Consequently, many TATs meet before or after school.

PERSPECTIVES

Multitudes of disruptions in every imaginable area can occur within the school setting. Some are nonviolent while others may be or may become violent. But all take their toll on the educational process and disrupt learning for more than one student. Numerous intervention strategies are available to combat disruptions and to ensure that the school will return to smooth functioning as soon as possible. Each school or district must develop its own plan of action. When an appropriate plan has been developed, crisis teams are frequently effective. On campus as well as off campus, general and special education personnel can become involved, and in all situations, parental notification is extremely essential.

The National Education Service Foundation developed plans to help curb violence among our nation's youth. Teenage health centers can help create a successful experience for students with problems. Schools can implement numerous policies for controlling disruptions on campus, including codes of conduct. Teachers, administrators, and staff need inservice training. Peer mediation, conflict mediation, and conflict resolution have been successful across schools. Care Teams are building-level teams who support and recommend services to students to reduce or eliminate their "at-riskness." Likewise, Student Assistance Teams function to intervene with students having problems, and Teacher Assistance Teams can help teachers deal with students with problems. Disruptions are inevitable, but well-planned interventions can help. Creating a safe, healthy school environment and establishing effective programs to help students experiencing problems can reduce disruptions and their consequences.

DISCUSSION QUESTIONS

1. List and briefly describe the types of disruption most likely to affect the school in which you work.

2. Describe possible intervention strategies that could be employed to effectively manage the disruptions you just listed.

3. Are any of the intervention strategies you just described currently included in your building and district crisis-intervention plans?

4. Examine the code of student conduct for your district or building. Which of the five options delineated in the section titled "Clarify and Publicize Student Code of Conduct" are employed? Are the options used in your district or building adequate? Why or why not?

5. Design a 30-minute faculty inservice describing one or more disruptions that could realistically affect your building and possible intervention strategies which could be employed.

CHAPTER 3

DISASTER

As we noted in Chapter 1, disasters are calamitous events that range from catastrophic property or personal injuries to loss of life. Disaster frequently involves community-wide devastation. Natural disasters—occurrences in nature over which humanity has little or no control—include tornadoes, hurricanes, floods, earthquakes, and fires. As Cornell (1982) points out

> The United States has gradually developed programs aimed at reducing or minimizing the effects of disaster on life and property through research into the causes and possible prediction of national disasters. Some of these efforts have been extremely successful, particularly the physical studies of disaster phenomena and the establishment of warning systems for weather events; other efforts have not been as successful, as in the case of long-term sociological and psychological studies. (p. 22)

Cornell explained *tornadoes* as "localized atmospheric storms of short duration and extreme violence associated with thunderstorms. Tornado winds form a whirlpool-like column of air rotating around a hollow center in which centrifugal force produces a partial vacuum" (p. 33). Nearly every spring, a tornado hits a school somewhere in the United States. Although many tornadoes occur in the late afternoon or early evening, that is, after school hours, others hit with little warning while the school is in session. Flying glass, falling roofs, and disappearing walls create havoc, destruction, injury, and even death. Putting the school back together is a daunting task. Buildings need to be rebuilt and classes have to be relocated. Materials may or may not be salvageable. After an experience like this, each time a storm approaches, all students including those with exceptionalities become upset and school is again disrupted.

Hurricanes are "severe tropical cyclones originating in warm ocean areas and generating winds of sustained velocities over 74 miles an hour" (Cornell,

1982, p. 35). Cornell added that "by any measure, the hurricane is the most powerful of all natural forces" (p. 35), and that "more than any other natural hazard affecting the United States, hurricanes in recent years have been characterized by a decreasing loss of life coupled with rapidly rising loss of property" (p. 36). Hurricanes can debilitate schools. When a hurricane is approaching, schools usually close to minimize loss of property or life within school buildings. Some schools include, just in case, an emergency shelter for students, teachers, and administrators when the storm hits. Although either measure helps prevent loss of life, the emotional shock may not be prevented. Even when a school is inland, severe weather such as high winds and tornadoes may be disastrous. If it is near the coastal waters, tidal waves may damage the school. Materials, furniture, and books could be damaged, all of which hampers the school's normal functioning.

"Almost every community in the United States suffers from some flooding problem, primarily caused by the runoff from heavy storms. ... The average annual number of flood deaths is still relatively low" (Cornell, 1982, p. 31). The damage to property, however, can be intense. In many communities, *floods* damage schools on a continuing basis. Therefore, current laws should prevent a new school from being built in a flood plain. Schools can also become flooded from dams or flood walls collapsing or from excessive rains. When a threat of a flood can be predicted, loss of life within the school can be averted, but the flood damage due to filthy water cannot be. Flood waters frequently damage floors, walls, desks, and materials. Mudslides from flood waters or excessive rains can also damage schools. Even when a school escapes or repairs flood damage, students may have to attend school while their homes are still flooded or damaged. Media pictures of floods in the Midwest in 1993 and 1995 showed students taking boats to school because roads in their flooded neighborhoods were still covered with water. In so many flood situations, students and teachers continually have the tragedy on their minds.

Cornell (1982) remarked that *earthquakes* "are among nature's most destructive and awesome phenomena" (p. 38). He wrote:

Perhaps more than any other natural disaster, the earthquake also has the potential to disrupt completely the fragile socioeconomic web of modern urban life, shattering all communications and life-support systems both above and below ground and disrupting vital services for days, weeks, even months. The complex network of family and community relationships also can be altered irreparably, as the physical and psychological trauma of the earthquake wipes out familiar landmarks and guideposts, forever changing the environment. (p. 38)

Earthquakes can occur at any time and in many parts of the world. They cannot be predicted, and to some extent loss of life, injury, and disruption are commonplace. Long periods of after-shocks also cause great concern as was noted after the 1994 earthquake in Los Angeles, California. Preparing students with exceptionalities to deal with earthquakes poses a great challenge because "most of these students have difficulty learning as early and comprehensively as other people. Many do not readily understand concepts presented in the abstract. Often the ability to generalize from experience is absent or generally reduced" (Muccigrosso et al., 1991, p. 6).

Other natural disasters are *medical* in nature. The AIDS virus infects more and more people. Because its devastating effects are felt everywhere, it has become a natural disaster. If youth without disabilities tend not to consider the long-term consequences of contacting AIDS and other sexually transmitted diseases (STDs), how can youth with disabilities be convinced of the dangers of STDs? Other diseases like the Ebola virus can also have disastrous effects on communities. Although this virus has primarily affected individuals in other countries, an outbreak or epidemic of the Ebola virus could strike in the U.S., especially in families or neighborhoods where medical assistance is expensive and not readily available. What would be the impact of such an outbreak or threat of one on individuals with exceptionalities? What kind of education would they need? Remember, an epidemic of any kind can become disastrous when necessary precautions are neglected and ignored. Muccigrosso et al. (1991) note that, in general,

Learning characteristics, together with significant social skills deficits (i.e., poor communication and decision-making skills, a limited socialization repertoire, and low self-esteem), increase the special education student's vulnerability to sexual abuse as well as unwanted pregnancy, premature parenthood, and sexually transmitted disease, including human immuno–deficiency virus (HIV). (p. 7)

Physical plant failures can lead to disasters and may be brought about by natural occurrence, mechanical malfunction, or utility disfunction of the facility (Mehring, 1995). The scope of the crisis can range from a minor inconvenience to a terrible catastrophe that includes property damage, injury, or the loss of life. Mehring divided disasters into major and minor categories. She considered broken pipes, the loss of air conditioning or heat, and the loss of utilities minor types of disaster. These may cause a disruption but usually not for long periods of time. Generally, they do not cause serious harm or injury. With broken water pipes or loss of heat in mid-winter, schools may need to be excused for a day or two, but usually everything is normal after that. Unfortunately, major disasters are much more disruptive. These include the spillage of hazardous materials, explosions, fire, live downed electrical wires, or gas leaks. These are major because of the longer term damage and the unfortunate possibility of injury and even death, especially to some individuals with disabilities.

Chemicals or hazardous materials have devastating effects on people. Let us assume, for instance, that chemicals placed in protective containers were being removed for disposal from a high school chemistry lab. The person carrying the containers trips and drops one. The container comes open, and a poisonous vapor fills the hallway and several classrooms. Students and teachers would be overcome and many might need emergency room treatment.

Another major threat to life and property is *fire* which "kills some 12,000 people in the United States each year, over 2,000 of them children. One American dies from fire every forty-four minutes. Most of these fires are small, localized fires, usually affecting a single home or apartment" (Cornell, 1982, p. 320). Fires in schools, hospitals, institutions, and hotels are frequently of catastrophic levels. Cornell confirmed that "loss of life is certain to increase as more and more business and residential property is concentrated into large multiple-storied building complexes" (p. 321). Section 504 of the Vocational Rehabilitation Act of 1973 (Public Law 93-112) and Americans with Disabilities Act of 1990 (Public Law 101-336) are laws that challenge public and private sectors to make their buildings accessible and facilities responsive to the needs of individuals with exceptionalities. The question is, How far have schools, homes, and businesses gone to provide measures for handling crises resulting from fires? When a school is burned by a fire, whether it is totally destroyed or can be repaired, problems exist. In addition to the materials burned, water or smoke damage is prevalent. Fires have many causes but in the majority of school buildings, they frequently are the result of arson. This becomes a serious problem for general and special educators. Schools in remote forest areas may also be threatened by forest fires. For example, a car hit the electrical transformer providing electricity to a trailer court close to an elementary school in Emporia, Kansas. The surge protector was knocked off, thus sending high voltage throughout the area. Immediately, some trailers and school property burst into flames. People were only able to save themselves but no belongings. Ten children from the court who attended the nearby school were affected. The school raised money and collected clothes, furniture, and supplies for the affected families.

Additionally, disasters can be deliberately caused by humans, and the results can be even more devastating for children and youth than those caused by natural disasters or accidents. Consider the terrorist bombing of the Federal Building in Oklahoma City in April 1995 already alluded to in Chapter 1. This type of disaster is more difficult to deal with because no reasonable or logical explanation exists for its inhuman action. The long-lasting fears, mental images, and horrors are difficult to assuage. One can take precautions against natural disasters, but it is much more difficult to do so against terrorists because the place and time of their strike is nearly always unexpected and unpredicted.

IMPACT OF DISASTER ON STUDENTS WITH EXCEPTIONALITIES

The effects of disaster can have far-reaching impacts on individuals with disabilities, and disasters, in themselves, can result in disabilities (e.g., serious fire burns, injuries due to earthquakes and terrorist bomb injuries). Two questions come to mind: How prepared are persons with exceptionalities to deal with disasters both on school campuses and in their respective communities? Also, how prepared are general and special educators to tackle disasters before, during, and after their occurrences?

For students with cognitive disabilities and those with physical and/or health impairments, disasters can pose insurmountable challenges, especially when they do not have self-help, coping, independent-living, and survival skills. Consider the following cases:

1. Steven was an average to low-average student whose father farmed in rural Kansas. Because of the devastating effects of a flood, his father filed for bankruptcy. The economic and financial strain on the family affected Steven who later developed emotional/behavior and learning problems. When invited to school, his parents did not attend. Steven was suspended several times from school and later expelled without procedural safeguards.

2. Christina was a student with gifts and talents. Her father was a rich farmer until the drought and heat wave affected his cows, and the majority of them died. Her father had problems with the insurance and was not adequately compensated. He began to consume excessive quantities of alcohol and the whole family was in tremendous crisis. The parents subsequently divorced and Student Y eventually dropped out of school.

3. James was a fifth grade student with a physical disability resulting from a doctor's drug recommendation during his mother's pregnancy. His school building was not accessible to persons with physical disability. In fact, the elevator malfunctioned frequently. One afternoon, there was a fire in his school and it was very difficult for his peers and teacher to move him out of the school building.

4. An interrelated special education program was located in a trailer that had little communication with the main school building. There was a sudden announcement of a tornado and in no time, the tornado touched down. The students, with different exceptionalities, tried to get to the main building that has a basement, but it was too late. Many of the students were injured.

5. A special education program was housed in a dilapidated building in one California city. During the night, this building was destroyed by an earthquake. This event disrupted students' programs for many weeks.

As these cases, both hypothetical and actual, illustrate, disasters can be extremely disruptive to the normal functioning of all students, and they can take a special toll on students with special needs. As a consequence, programs should focus on enhancing coping and survival skills. In Case #1, the devastation of the flood affected the family and the student. General and special educators must provide counseling that empowers both parents and students in collaborative, consultative, and cooperative fashions. When students have problems, they need support and not suspension and expulsion from school programs. Procedural safeguards must be taken seriously. Case #2 shows how many students with gifts and talents are ignored in school programs. There is the outrageous assumption that they are "super kids" who come from "super homes." Christina dropped out of school because of tremendous family stress and crises. To prevent this, general and special educators and the parents must form a partnership in solving crisis situations before the student drops out. Opportunities for redemption should always be available to all students, irrespective of their exceptionalities.

In Case #3, James's physical disability was downplayed and that placed him in an at-risk situation. For persons with exceptionalities, general and special educators should focus on (a) honoring their civil rights, that is, respecting their equal protection under the law; (b) eliminating all barriers that impede survival and success; (c) making programs accessible; and (d) making employability possible. Case #4 deals with problems associated with divorcing special education programs from the general flow of school programs. Again, prescriptions for Case #3 are useful in dealing with Case #4. In Case #5, the dilapidated building that housed special education classes collapsed as a result of the earthquake. Programs that enhance students' self-concept and coping skills must be instituted immediately to reduce the long-term effects of the earthquake. Again, an empowering partnership between the home, school, and community is needed.

INTERVENTION STRATEGIES FOR DISASTER

As indicated earlier, disaster frequently involves community-wide devastation. Hurricanes, tornadoes, earthquakes, fires, floods, and bombs inflict sudden damage that is irreversible and sometimes widespread. Disaster survivors experience danger and loss of control. Recovery from a disaster involves a lengthy process requiring the individual to develop an ability to deal with long-term stress and fear. In children and youth, fear is often expressed through several behaviors including anxiety, hyperactivity, flashbacks, nervousness, undue cautiousness, and/or separation anxiety. Stomachaches and headaches are common psychologically based complaints, especially among young children. Truancy often increases in adolescents. Students who display these behaviors several months after the disaster may suffer from post-traumatic stress disorder. Petersen and Straub (1992) recommend the use of a crisis trainer, team leader, system-wide crisis team, teacher time and attention, and clean-up activities. These recommendations are discussed next.

Crisis Trainer

Because disasters frequently affect more than one school within a system, one individual counselor, school psychologist, or social worker should be designated as the crisis trainer for each building. The crisis trainer determines the type of assistance children or youth may need. He or she consults with building administrators and teachers to develop plans of action for assisting students and staff to deal with the aftermath of the disastrous crisis.

Team Leader

When a disaster strikes, a district level person should be designated to network with each crisis trainer. This Team Leader assists crisis trainers in coordinating needed district resources and serves as an advisor and advocate to the school board.

System-Wide Crisis Team

Whenever a disaster is widespread, crisis support beyond what can be provided by the crisis trainer should be given to students and staff members requiring it. A system-wide crisis team should include district personnel trained in consultation and counseling. Depending on need, community mental health professionals may also be involved.

Teacher Time and Attention

Given the pervasiveness of disasters, teachers sometimes suffer from loss of possessions, homes, or loved ones. If schools are closed due to the disaster's damage (physical or psychological), teachers and other staff can use this time to establish contacts with coworkers and begin to deal with the stress. Classrooms may also be in disarray or relocated after a disaster. Scheduling planning time prior to reopening will allow teachers to organize classroom lessons, instructional activities, and one-on-one response to student fears.

Preventive and Clean-Up Activities

Restoring a sense of control after a disaster is crucial to the recovery process. Petersen and Straub (1992) cite the example of a teacher in Charleston, South Carolina, who engaged students in building birdhouses to replace those destroyed by Hurricane Hugo. This activity gave students responsibility for assisting with clean-up activities and provided a rehabilitative opportunity to be in control.

Prior to an earthquake, students and school personnel who live in earthquake prone areas should receive instruction regarding appropriate action to take should an earthquake occur. Cornell (1982) recommends instruction on how to remain calm and carefully think through every action. Seeking immediate protection from falling debris by taking cover in a doorway or under a sturdy table or desk is an intervention strategy that should be rehearsed and practiced. Individuals need to be taught to stay away from windows, staircases, and elevators during the earthquake. If outside the school building, students and staff should be instructed to seek protection in the nearest doorway and to avoid high buildings, walls, power poles, and other tall structures.

It is highly unlikely that a school will, on short notice, experience flooding. It is, however, possible that staff and students engaged in a field trip or extracurricular activity could find themselves in a situation where flooding may occur. Cornell (1982) suggests immediate evacuation while attending to advisories issued by the National Weather Service and Corps of Engineers (or agency responsible for flood control in the area) concerning flood stages and evacuation routes. Flooded areas, including bridges, dams, and levees along the flooding waterway, should be avoided. If evacuation is not possible, there should be a plan for moving students to higher ground or upper floors if in a building. Intervention also includes waiting for waters to recede or for rescue team assistance rather than attempting escape by foot or vehicle.

Instruction in hurricane emergency procedures should be provided to all students and school staff in hurricane-prone areas. During the hurricane season (i.e., from June 1 to November 30), the school principal should make daily checks of area weather forecasts and disseminate appropriate information to staff and students. Possible evacuation routes and/or school dismissal procedures should be planned in advance. According to Cornell (1982), "in the event of a hurricane, evacuation to a good shelter far away from shorelines can increase survival chances to nearly 100 percent" (p. 90). If evacuation prior to the hurricane is not possible, students and staff should remain inside the school building until advised that the danger has passed. Under no circumstances should school personnel or students go outside or to beach or bay areas until the danger has passed. Once the storm is over, caution should be exercised when walking or driving because roadways, breakwalls, and bridges may have sustained damage by waves and wind. Additional hazards include fallen power lines and poisonous snakes which may have sought shelter on high ground or under buildings.

Unfortunately, the warning period for a tornado is often so short that the best prevention strategy is to seek immediate cover. Each school building should designate a basement or ground floor area near the center of the building away from windows as the official tornado shelter. Corridors facing north are the safest; those facing east are second best. All individuals should immediately evacuate large rooms (e.g., gymnasiums, cafeterias, and auditoriums) with free ceilings. If students and staff are caught outdoors in the event of a tornado, they should be instructed to lie down flat in the nearest depression, ditch, or ravine.

POST-TRAUMATIC STRESS DISORDER

After disasters, most teachers and students usually are on the road to recovery within a few days to a few weeks. For some, the aftershock of a tragedy may last for years. It is important for general and special educators to recognize the symptoms of post-traumatic stress disorder (PTSD) and become aware of interventions which may assist an individual to overcome this disorder. More importantly, educators need to be aware of ways to prevent PTSD from occurring, and to avoid iatrogenic intervention, that is, solving a problem that does not exist. PTSD symptoms include

1. Recurrent and intrusive recollections of the event.

2. Nightmares.

3. Numbing of emotions.

4. Marked disinterest in activities.

5. Feelings of detachment.

6. Hypervigilant or avoidance behavior.

7. Decline in cognitive performance.

8. Startled reactions.

9. Overwhelming and persistent guilt.

10. Distortion of time concerning the incident.

11. Distortion of the sequence of events.

12. Repetitive play involving traumatic themes.

13. Pessimistic expectations of the future and lifespan.

14. Enduring personality changes. (Petersen & Straub, 1992)

Two techniques, defusing and debriefing, may assist students and staff in constructively dealing with PTSD to avoid devastation. *Defusing* engages individuals in venting thoughts and emotions immediately following the tragic event, preferably before leaving school the day of the event. Students and parents should be informed of possible reactions (e.g., sleeplessness, nausea, irritability, fear, and anxiety). They should be told that these reactions are "normal," and suggestions for coping should be shared. According to Petersen and Straub (1992), *debriefing* can involve students in a 6-phase process during which students examine questions appropriate for each stage:

1. *Information Phase.*

   • What happened?

   • Where were you?

   • What role did you play?

2. *Idea Phase.*

   • What thoughts have you had?

   • What ideas did you think of?

3. *Emotional Phase.*

   • How did you react at first?

   • How are you reacting now?

   • What impact has this had on you? (Note: Expressing emotions through crying, anger, fear, and so forth is encouraged.)

4. *Meaning Phase.*

   • What repercussions has this had on your life?

   • What symptoms are you experiencing?

   • How has this affected your family, school, health, and friends?

5. *Educational Phase.*

   • How have you coped with difficulties before?

   • What are you doing to cope now?

6. *Closure.* In this phase, individuals are reminded and reassured about the healing process. Therapeutic sessions must

   • Remind students of strengths.

   • Reassure students it will take time to heal.

   • Reassure students that you will be there. (p. 98)

as a sunny and warm spring day after an especially harsh winter. sophomores skipped school and went joy riding. They tried ing a train but did not make it.

ne boys were horsing around in the locker room after their physi- education class. They pushed on the lockers that then went mbling over, killing another student changing his clothes on the her side.

homas was angry with his parents and ran away from home. Later at night he was beaten and robbed and left in a field. A heavy now fell during the night and his body was not found for two days. When a violent act occurs, interventions need to include safety and security issues.

Two teachers and a principal from the same elementary school died during the same academic year. All the employees were well liked but the third one to die, the fourth grade teacher, was especially admired by many. The staff and students became traumatized.

A high school student dressed in camouflage entered the gymnasium during an assembly. He gunned down an assistant principal and three students before he was knocked to the ground. Gun safety and the dangers of weapons needed to be discussed.

10. The death of a national figure, such as Christie McAuliffe, causes widespread distress. Thus, the death of President John F. Kennedy traumatized the nation, and its effect is still felt today. Most Ameri- cans over the age of 40 remember what they were doing the day President Kennedy was assassinated. Similarly, most Americans will probably remember the day of the Oklahoma bombing not only because of the horrible nature of the crisis but also because of the tremendous loss of lives.

Suicide

Adolescent *suicide* has tripled over the past decade (Kirk, 1993; Woolfolk, 1993) and is now the third most common cause of death among adolescents. Some

PERSPECTIVES

Disasters may be natural (e.g., hurricanes, tornadoes, floods, or earthquakes) or caused by humans (e.g., fires or bombs). They may result in property de- struction, injury, and even death. Regardless, they cause serious problems for schools, general and special education personnel, students, parents, and com- munities.

Crisis teams need to respond to a disaster and its results with swiftness and thoroughness. Preplanned responses are often necessary. Specified per- sonnel need to lead others through the crisis response (e.g., school build- ing or district wide plans). It is important that general and special educa- tors understand the important role they play in helping students work through the effects of a crisis. Practitioners and administrators must also understand that PTSD frequently occurs and that recovery can take a long time. Defusing and debriefing are key strategies that can be put into proper use to help those so inflicted.

DISCUSSION QUESTIONS

1. List and briefly describe the types of disaster most likely to affect the school in which you work.

2. Describe possible intervention strategies that could be employed to effectively manage the disasters you just listed.

3. Which of the intervention strategies you just described are included in your building and district crisis-intervention plans?

4. How can you assist students to effectively deal with post-traumatic stress disorder?

5. Design a 30-minute faculty inservice describing one or more disasters that could realistically affect your building and possible intervention strategies.

DEATH

Death generally has a profound effect on those a
Effects are evident when the death is that of a fello
member, a relative of a student, an important con
tional figure. The type of death can also influence
acts resulting in death may tend to produce a grea
Consider the following cases:

1. When Jason was in the third grade, he was pre.
   ther fell from a tree while cutting branches and
   person who has died is very close to the child or
   present when the death occurred, discussions nee
   a great deal of emphasis does not have to be place
   rence with all members of the class.

2. When Claudia was in the fifth grade, her mother di
   dents in the class feared the death of their own parer
   knowledge that children react with fear and question
   existence when death occurs. They may want to leave
   check on their parents. The fear of losing their own pa
   Claudia's classmates to isolate and exclude her.

3. Loi was diagnosed with leukemia when she was 13 years
   died two years later. Many of her classmates became con
   about getting cancer as well. Children and adolescents nee
   reassured that this is generally unlikely.

4. Christian had strep throat but his busy parents thought it wa
   minor and did not seek medical treatment. Christian died. C
   and youth have to be counseled into (a) knowing about preve.
   strategies and appropriate medicines and (b) seeking proper m
   treatment and good health care.

5. It wa
   Fou
   bea

6. Sor
   cal
   tu
   ot

7. T
   t
   s

8.

researchers believe that some accidents may be suicide. According to Pitcher and Poland (1993), about 10% of children between the ages of 6 and 12 have *depression* severe enough to interfere with daily functioning and nearly one-half of these consider and even dwell on committing suicide. General and special educators, service providers, and parents need to be concerned about suicide when an individual displays some of the following signs:

1. Difficulty sleeping and eating appropriately.
2. Pervasive feeling of hopelessness and helplessness.
3. Difficulty concentrating, lethargy, and difficulty completing tasks.
4. Withdrawal.
5. Anger, aggressiveness, and poor social adjustment.
6. Low self-esteem, self-deprecating remarks, extreme sensitivity to making mistakes, and repeatedly behaving in a manner that brings about negative consequences. (Pitcher & Poland, 1993, p. 16)

Eggen and Kauchak (1994) report that 5,000 youths die from suicide each year and experts estimate that for every successful suicide there are 50 to 100 attempts. Suicide often comes as a response to life problems–problems that parents and teachers sometimes dismiss. A few years ago, Salkind (1990) suggested that the causes of teenage suicide, while complex, are related to a number of conditions including family turmoil, depression, drug or alcohol abuse, underachievement, alienation from peers and society, and child abuse.

Berk (1991) and Rosenthal and Rosenthal (1984) describe two types of students who attempt suicide. One is the academically oriented student with high personal standards who is solitary, withdrawn, and self-critical. More common is the low-achieving, impulsive student who has low self-esteem and little tolerance for stress and frustration. Berk further described several factors linked to the actual occurrence of suicide. One is the break-up of a peer relationship; another is problems in school or with the law. For the isolated or egocentric teenager, the shame and humiliation that occur when these problems are revealed to parents often seem too much to bear. A third factor is exposure to suicide–one third to one half of suicide victims knew someone who attempted or completed suicide.

Consider the following cases:

1. Herman was a typical teenager. He was quiet, had few friends, and did not want many interactions with adults. He went out walking about 9 o'clock one dark night and was run over and killed by a truck. Initially, it was thought to be an accident until a note was found in his locker detailing his feelings of rejection and hopelessness.

2. Brett was not a very popular or well-known boy and he had difficulty in school. He pulled out a gun and shot himself in front of the English class, a class he was failing. Trauma overtook the entire class and school.

3. A major concern in schools is cluster suicides where one student commits suicide followed by copycat suicides. Robbie, Derick, and Jason were best of friends who did everything together. Jason went away for the summer to work in a resort. Robbie and Derick suddenly and without warning committed suicide together. They both shot themselves in the temple. Soon after their funeral, Jason attempted suicide in the same manner but shot too far forward. Although he did not die, he was blinded. Kirk (1993) explains that cluster suicides appear to be geographically linked. Also, they appear to be a part of the contagious vulnerability of adolescence. When a teenage suicide occurs, the school needs to take steps to prevent copycat ones.

DEVELOPMENTAL UNDERSTANDING OF DEATH

The developmental age of a child, not the chronological age, influences how the child reacts to someone's death. The age of understanding also determines the reaction to an intervention strategy.

Young Children

Younger children tend not to be as affected by death as are older children and youth (Petersen & Straub, 1992). Children *younger than five* seldom have an understanding of the finality of death. Rather, separation is the pain the child feels. Television, especially cartoons, demonstrates that a person can be hurt, maimed, or killed on one show and show up fine in the next. Death is, therefore, not a reality. Often a *child of five* will re-experience the grief of death around age eight when the concept of the person never coming back is finally understood. Experiences of loss must be discussed when the concept of finality is understood (Petersen & Straub, 1992). For example, Linda's mother died when Linda was five. Linda seemed to adjust well, behaved properly in school, and obtained good grades. When she was eight, her school work began to deteriorate and she started to have behavior problems. Linda had reached the developmental age where she could finally understand the finality of her mother's death, and she was having problems adjusting to her new understanding.

During the developmental level of *six to eight,* children tackle the concept of living and nonliving, and some may develop a morbid curiosity about death. A child at this level may kill a bug, watch it for a while, and suddenly exclaim "It is still dead!" Such experimentation gives the child needed information about life and death and about the reality and finality of death. Some children become fascinated not only with death but with the rituals surrounding death. A child may be distraught one moment and the next ask probing questions. If adults are not comfortable discussing death with the child and communicate nonverbal messages, the questions will stop and the child will be forced to resolve the trauma and find answers in isolation. This can result in much misinformation.

Children in the development age period of *eight to twelve years* begin to understand that they will never see their loved ones again. Their grief includes not only the separation of the moment but the pain of forever. Also, the self-centered thinking patterns typical of this age level lead children to believe they have control over the world or reality. They do not understand that people react to behavior but that the behavior is not the cause of the reaction (Petersen & Straub, 1992). For instance, Bill and Jim had sibling problems. In the heat of anger, Bill wished Jim were dead—he even prayed for it. Two weeks later, Jim was hit by a car and died. Bill felt very guilty because he believed he was the cause of Jim's death.

Early Teenage Years

The child in *middle-school or junior-high-school age* reacts somewhat differently. This age group easily becomes involved in the sensationalization of death. Oftentimes, students' reactions will be defiant humor to show they are not affected. Because early teenagers are so emotional, extreme emotional outbursts such as anger will occur, and steps need to be instituted to head off these outbursts.

As abstract thinking begins at about age 12, the teenager begins to understand the finality of death much as an adult does. However, teenagers claim their own invincibility. Although they know differently, they believe death claims only the elderly. Often, when a teenager dies, this belief is shattered and other teenagers go into a mortality crisis (Petersen & Straub, 1992). Their response can be either healthy or unhealthy. Following are central issues that need to be discussed at this juncture:

1. How to bring meaning to life.

2. Why death strikes young people.

3. What occurs after death.

4. How to rebuild personal foundations after a tragedy.

The teenager with a healthy emotional makeup who experiences the death of another young person often chooses a career focused on solving problems related to the death. The belief is injustice was done, and the philosophy is, "I will make the world right." For instance, Juanita and Maria were best friends since kindergarten. Marie contracted Hodgkins Disease when she was a freshman in high school and died two years later. Juanita set a goal to go to medical school and become a doctor so she could find a cure for this horrible cancer. Sometimes, a teenager who does not have a solid emotional foundation will react to a friend or peer's death as if he or she will also soon be wiped from the face of the earth so there is no need to study today. Unfortunately, this teenager may turn to substance abuse, sexual promiscuity, dropping out of school, or suicide.

AGE-SPECIFIC REACTIONS TO DEATH

Petersen and Straub (1992) stated that there are age-specific reactions to someone's death. Children aged 6 to 10 frequently express themselves through play, art, and music. Their reactions include

- Reduced attention span.
- Radical, out-of-character changes in behavior.
- Fantasies that include a savior at the end.
- Mistrust of adults.

Girls aged 10 to 12 and boys aged 12 to 14 are still childlike in attitude. Their reactions can include

- Anger at unfairness.
- Excitement at own survival.
- Attribution of symbolic meaning to events (omens).
- Self-judgments.
- Psychosomatic illnesses.

Girls aged 13 to 18 and boys aged 15 to 18 have reactions similar to adults. The reactions include

- Judgmental reasoning as to the causes of the events.
- Mortality crises.
- Move to adult responsibilities to assume control.
- Suspicious and guarded reactions.
- Eating and sleeping disorders.
- Alcohol and drug abuse.
- Loss of impulse control. (Petersen & Straub, 1992, p. 71)

Schools are sometimes unaware of the emotional upheavals in a student's life because he or she may not want to share a problem or may want to protect the family. Oftentimes, a crisis will bring these problems forward for discussion. For example, Minh was abused at home but never mentioned it to anyone. A classmate, Jose, committed suicide. As the class discussed Jose's problems, Minh was finally able to mention his abuse.

A variety of symptoms such as shock, feelings of helplessness, and disbelief may be felt by individuals unable to resolve the crises they face in life and to return balance to their lives. Often denial, or refusing to believe something bad has really happened, is an individual's reaction to loss. Sooner or later, however, he or she has to acknowledge that a significant event or loss has occurred. Not being able to control the outcome of an event can create helpless feelings (Lindemann, 1944; Smith, 1989). For example, Smith highlighted reactions accompanying death to include "somatic distress; preoccupation with the image of the deceased; guilt; hostile reactions; and loss of patterns of conduct" (p. 6). A half century earlier, Lindemann (1944) identified characteristics of those mourning for the death of someone to include

1. The marked tendency to sighing respiration—this respiration disturbance was most conspicuous when the patient was made to discuss his or her grief.

2. The complaint about lack of strength and exhaustion which is universal and is described as follows: "It is almost impossible to climb up a stairway."

3. Digestive symptoms, described as follows: "The food tastes like sand." (pp. 141-142)

DEATH-RELATED CRISES: IMPACT ON STUDENTS WITH EXCEPTIONALITIES

Children and adolescents with physical, emotional, and cognitive disabilities are at higher risk for depression and suicide than youngsters without disabilities (Guetzloe, 1991). Suicidal behavior has been noted in children with mental disabilities as well as children with superior intelligence (Pfeffer, 1981). Children with exceptionalities may often suffer from feelings of hopelessness, helplessness, and low self-esteem, which may increase their vulnerability to suicidal behaviors (Peck, 1985; Pfeffer, 1986). In addition, students with disabilities have been found to be disproportionately susceptible to abuse, which in turn may trigger suicidal thoughts and actions (Guetzloe, 1989). Blumenthal (1990) estimated that over 90% of suicidal children and youth, have associated, serious psychiatric illnesses that include conduct disorder, depression or bipolar illness, abuse of drugs or alcohol, and psychosis. Depression in particular has been found to be a primary risk factor related to suicidal behavior in children and youth. Even though a student may not meet the criteria to receive specific education and/or related services, health, cognitive, and social/emotional difficulties which can be remediated through other school or community-based intervention programs may be identified.

Many studies have confirmed that children and adolescents with depressive disorders are at high risk for suicidal behavior (Cohen-Sandler, Berman, & King, 1982; Dyer & Kreitman, 1984; Pfeffer & Plutchick, 1982; Pfeffer, Zuckerman, Plutchick, & Mizruchi, 1984; Robbins & Alessi, 1985). Depression can be reliably diagnosed in children as young as 6 to 8 years of age (Guetzloe, 1991). Estimates of the prevalence of depression among children and youth with learning and/or behavioral problems tend to be higher than those cited for the general population. Forness (1988) and Mattison, Humphrey, Kales, Hernit, and Finkenbinder (1986) reported that approximately 50% of the special education population may have symptoms of depression in addition to other difficulties such as learning disabilities or behavioral disorders. Pfeffer (1986) recommends that children evaluated for any type of psychiatric disorder, in particular, should also be evaluated for depression and suicidal tendencies.

Earlier on, Brumback, Statton, and Wilson (1980) observed that children with learning disabilities may be at risk for both depression and suicidal behavior. Peck (1985) reported that 50% of all children under 15 who committed suicide over a 3-year period in Los Angeles, California, had been diagnosed as having a learning disability. Guetzloe (1989) reported that high rates of depression, self-destructive behavior, and suicidal tendencies have been noted among children diagnosed as either deaf or hearing impaired. These students may suffer from isolation and may have difficulties in understanding and expressing feelings. In addition, children with medical problems often face extreme and/or chronic stress which places them at risk for depression (Stark, 1990). Estimates of depression among children with medical problems range from 7% in general medical patients to 23% in orthopedic patients (Guetzloe, 1991).

A variety of assessment models, checklists, observational outlines, and clinical tests are now readily available for school psychologists trained in interviewing techniques and psychoeducational assessments. Input should be sought from general and special educators; counselors; parents; and, if appropriate, psychologists; psychiatrists; and/or other medical personnel. The primary focus of an IEP for a student at risk for suicide should be on ameliorating symptoms of depression and suicidal behavior with remediation of academic deficits becoming secondary, at least for the time being. Family education (including counseling or therapy) should be included in the IEP as a related service. General and special educators must discuss affordable community resources (e.g., community mental health centers, psychiatric hospitals, health and human service agencies, and private psychologists) that provide assessment and treatment for depressed and suicidal youth. Additionally, they must not be afraid to query students about suicidal threats or statements. The more detailed and lethal a student's plan is, the more critical it is to immediately notify the school contact person, who will notify the parent(s) and appropriate community personnel. Such a student ought to be kept under close supervision and *never* be left alone. According to Guetzloe (1991),

> The primary roles of school personnel (general and special education) are to detect the signs of suicide and potential suicide, to make immediate referrals to the contact person within the school, to notify parents, to secure assistance from school and community resources, and to assist, as members of the support team, in follow-up activity after a suicide threat or attempt. (p. 23)

All general and special educators and service providers should receive training in crisis counseling as a component of preservice and/or inservice instruction. Such training should include techniques to effectively (a) handle a depression or suicide-related behavior; (b) adapt classroom-management procedures to emphasize support, encouragement, gains, and accomplishments; and (c) design classroom intervention strategies which focus on cognitive flexibility, hopefulness, strong social supports, removal from stressors, self-worth, security, and self-control (Guetzloe, 1991). When dealing with students with exceptionalities, one size never fits all. For example, unless general and special educators are prepared to work with students with hearing or language impairments, individual and group counseling may be of limited value. Also, specially trained therapists will make greater gains using play therapy with students who have cognitive disabilities (Webb, 1991). An intervention plan stressing bibliotherapy with students who have learning disabilities may be the best approach when ability-appropriate materials are employed. In short, care should be taken to select intervention approaches compatible with the cognitive, emotional, learning, and physical needs of each student.

INTERVENTION STRATEGIES FOR DEATH-RELATED CRISES

Some death-related crises can be prevented, while some cannot. In all, the roles of general and special educators cannot be underestimated. Following are notable strategies for dealing with such crises.

Suicide

One crisis that can be prevented is suicide. As Clark-Stewart and Friedman (1987) point out, students contemplating suicide usually exhibit (a) changes in behavior at school such as skipping classes, missing assignments, or doing poorly on examinations; (b) personality changes such as moodiness, angry outbursts, or lack of concern about health or appearance; (c) possible drug or alcohol abuse; and (d) depression and withdrawal from friends, school activities, or both. General and special educators, administrators, parents, service providers, religious leaders, and businesses can help reduce suicide rates of students. For instance, teachers should be concerned about students who suddenly give away prize possessions such as pets, clothing, and collections and who show signs of depression or hyperactivity. Whenever a suicide is suspected, a teacher, counselor, or other concerned individual should talk to the student directly. A student who talks about suicide and has a plan for carrying it out is particularly at risk. Eight out of 10 people who commit suicide tell someone that they are thinking about hurting themselves before they actually do it. If a student talks about suicide, the best action is to listen carefully to what is being said and to take what is being expressed seriously. The suicidal student must be given a chance to express feelings and concerns. Students who talk about suicide are often confused about whether they want to live or die. Suicide is often intended as a cry for help. Responsible professionals must refer students contemplating suicide to counselors, school psychologists, school social workers, or others within the community who can provide the guidance and counseling needed to overcome the experiences and feelings which may have led to thoughts of suicide.

Suicide Prevention Strategies. As part of a crisis intervention plan, schools should develop a program to reduce the probability of a student choosing suicide as an option for coping with the varied stressors encountered, especially those occurring during the developmental years. Petersen and Straub (1992) suggest that an adequate suicide prevention program must seek to

1. Help teachers and counselors identify the broad spectrum of at-risk students.
2. Ensure that school personnel such as counselors will be available to help identified students (rather than tied up with tasks such as scheduling students, a frequent occurrence at the secondary level).
3. Diminish the predisposing conditions of the school community.
4. Increase the coping skills of students. (p. 143)

Woolfolk (1993) provides additional suggestions for suicide prevention such as (a) offering drama classes that focus on common teen problems, (b) providing help for coping with depression, (c) providing wallet cards that list coping skills and hot lines for help, and (d) providing peer counseling. The two most widely accepted and least controversial aspects of suicide prevention are (a) providing education for identification of high-risk students and (b) referral of these students for counseling (Petersen & Straub, 1992). Suicide training for school personnel must include

1. Information on acute and chronic risk factors for youth suicide.
2. Information on behavioral manifestations in the school setting of depression, schizophrenia, and conduct disorders.
3. Information and sources for referring students who are at risk.
4. Training in communication skills to approach and engage children at risk and their families.
5. Developing plans for school-system response to a student death or suicide.

6. Training in fostering the positive emotional development of youth and in realizing the importance of experiences to enhance self-concept.

Suicide Postvention Strategies. In the event that a suicide does occur, it is critical for schools to have a plan of action in place to prevent the possibility of a suicide cluster. Petersen and Straub (1992) cite the Center for Disease Control statistics indicating that suicide clusters account for between 1% and 5% of completed suicides. Given this possible aftermath, it is critical to handle a suicide with expertise and understanding. In the event of a school-related suicide, the school becomes a suicide survivor. Collectively, the school experiences all of the emotions (e.g., guilt, anger, anxiety, and denial) that individual survivors encounter. These intense emotional reactions are amplified by having so many people in one place who are survivors. An effective postsuicide plan should include (a) the identification of high-risk students, (b) a plan for announcing the death, (c) counseling for at-risk students, (d) a plan for allowing students to attend the funeral, (e) preparation of a response to the media, and (f) debriefing. Regular education teachers, special education teachers, coaches, counselors, and other school staff members must be prepared to identify the following high-risk students for suicide clusters in the event of a school-related suicide:

1. Relatives and close friends of the deceased.
2. Boyfriend or girlfriend of the deceased.
3. Pall bearers at the funeral.
4. Hospital visitors if the deceased had made previous attempts.
5. Students absent in the following week if not clearly excused for an illness.
6. People outside of the school having close involvement with the deceased.
7. Students with a history of depression.
8. Students with weak social supports.
9. Students who recently moved into the school.

10. Students with known family troubles.

11. Anyone involved in past or present suicide attempts.

Suicide evokes more complex emotions in survivors than any other form of death. Heightened emotions often result in distortion of facts and generation of rumors surrounding the suicide. Reports of the event are usually more graphic and gruesome than what actually occurred. To alleviate these reactions, a plan should be in place for informing school personnel about a school-related suicide. General and special educators should be told privately and given time to deal with their own emotions before sharing information with students. In addition to being informed about the suicide, school personnel should be provided information regarding where to send students, what to say to students, and what the funeral arrangements are. Because many individuals may be at risk once a suicide occurs, the school counseling department should be freed of other responsibilities so that they will have time to interact effectively with students referred for counseling. If large numbers of students are identified as at risk, additional counseling personnel may need to be called upon to assist. These personnel might include school psychologists, school social workers, personnel from other buildings within the district, and/ or community mental health professionals.

It is *not* advisable to hold a memorial service at the school in response to a suicide as it may dramatize and glorify the suicidal act. Students should be allowed, however, to attend funeral services as a means of working through the grief reaction process. Counseling should be available after the funeral service to any student who indicates an interest in talking with someone. Any memorializing that students want to do should be focused on helping survivors or on promoting healthy living skills. Suicide, especially that involving a student or school staff member, acts like a magnet for the media. Petersen and Straub (1992) offer the following suggestions for effectively working with the media in the case of a suicide:

1. When possible, use the district spokesperson to address the media.

2. Provide factual, not graphic, information.

3. Direct the press to other resources which can provide additional information on the topic of suicide.

4. Provide honest answers to questions.

5. Describe the plan of action in place and resources being used to effectively deal with the aftermath of the suicide.

6. Remind the media of consequences of sensationalizing a school-related suicide, especially one involving a student. (pp. 154-155)

It is evident that suicide touches many individuals. After a suicide, it is not uncommon for some individuals to experience guilt and fault for not recognizing the warning signs or taking a proactive role in preventing the individual from committing suicide. Debriefing is imperative! School personnel should be afforded the opportunity to discuss their emotions and reactions with trained personnel.

Terminal Illness

It is not unlikely that students, during the prekindergarten through 12th grade experience, will have a classmate or will know someone within the school environment (e.g., teacher, paraprofessional, custodian) who has a terminal illness. Often, the individual with the terminal illness undergoes significant physical, emotional, and perhaps behavioral changes as the illness progresses. Loss of hair, weight loss, irritability, depression, and other manifestations may be observed.

Parents and family members should be encouraged to provide as much factual information about the illness as possible to school personnel, and permission should be sought to share information, as needed, with staff members and students. Petersen and Straub (1992) recommend sharing information about the illness with students at a time when the affected individual is not present, especially if he or she is a peer. The discussion should begin by encouraging students to talk about any changes in the individual they may have observed (e.g., hair loss, weight loss, and skin color). Factual information about the illness should be provided, with special emphasis placed on the idea that the illness cannot be transmitted to others. Younger children may have to be reminded of the latter concept frequently. The potential for the individual's death should be discussed openly and honestly, allowing for student questions and concerns. The discussion should also engage students in discussing proactive strategies for interacting positively with the sick individual. Students should be guided toward treating the individual as normally as possible.

Death and the Grief Reaction Process

Suffering a serious loss in one's personal life can lead to behavioral and emotional problems and/or difficulty in academic and social skills. One means of assisting students to overcome their sense of loss is to understand the five stages of the grief reaction process. Petersen and Straub (1992) remarked that every person grieves somewhat differently and there is seldom any clear-cut order or pattern. One individual might move quickly from one emotion to the next while another might show only one intense emotion for a long period of time. A brief overview of each stage of grief and suggestions for helping individuals to deal with each stage are discussed next.

Denial Stage. An individual at this stage is intellectually aware that a loss has occurred but wants to believe and/or act as if the dead individual will return. Preserving a room or continuing shared rituals (e.g., a walk in the park on Sunday afternoons) may be observed as attempts to bring the individual back. Another common reaction during this stage is making deals. In this case, an individual might promise God that he or she will complete all chores without complaining if the loved one can be returned. A child or adolescent in the denial stage can appear to be a model student, son, or daughter–but only for a few weeks or months. Once it is recognized that all the good behavior in the world will not bring back the loved one, inconsistent behavior generally is observed.

Teachers, counselors, or others interacting with the child during the denial stage should not refute the expression of desire for the loved one's return. Identification of the emotion expressed–"you're really missing Jose, aren't you?"–will communicate understanding and acceptance. On the other hand, direct intervention is necessary when erratic behavior, hostility, depression, or a marked drop in grades are observed after a student experiences the loss of a significant other in his or her life. Petersen and Straub (1992) recommend working with the child on a scrapbook containing photographs or other memorabilia associated with the significant person.

Commemoratives might also assist the child to deal effectively with grief. For instance, when one of the authors was a young child, her grandfather always carried a smooth stone in his pocket. Whenever anyone was upset, the grandfather would remove the stone from his pocket and rub it until all the worry went away. Upon his death, the author carried this stone and rubbed away worries just as the grandfather had done.

A dream diary might provide an additional means of assisting students to deal effectively with denial. Dreams allow the unconscious mind to deal with loss. The child may report to a teacher or parent that he or she dreamed about the person who died. If this is a frequent occurrence, keeping a dream diary may assist the child to acknowledge in a healthy way the individual who is no longer present.

Fear Stage. Tragedies that involve violence often instill fear in survivors. Children, in particular, may fear that a similar fate may befall themselves, other family members, or close friends. Some children may be reluctant to return to school after the funeral, fearing that family members may also die before they return home from school. Allowing the child to remain home for a few days until a more normal family routine exists is often the best cure.

In cases where a classmate's death has resulted from shooting, kidnapping, and murder, providing a sense of assurance is critical to the healing process. Using developmentally appropriate instruction on how to protect oneself may help alleviate or at least minimize the fear reaction. Realistic discussions may also help to dispel this reaction to grief. Nightmares are often a component of the fear stage. Allowing students to discuss what they have dreamed alleviates fears that surround the incident. Even if no nightmares are reported, engaging students in a discussion about what happened (e.g., accident, suicide, shooting) allows a sense of control to be restored.

Anger Stage. Anger is the one emotion that survivors of loss, regardless of reason (e.g., divorce, old age, suicide, accident), universally feel. Individuals are angry at the person who has left them, perhaps at themselves for not doing something to prevent the loss, or at one or more other individuals for their perceived role in the loss. As Petersen and Straub (1992) point out, "individuals who are at the anger stage search for someone or something to blame and thereby justify their angry attacks" (p. 81).

A critical role played by general and special educators is to direct the anger into constructive activity. Students should be taught that, while they may not be able to control the emotion they feel, they can control what they do with those feelings. Physical activities (e.g., swimming, running, dancing) and creative activities (e.g., entries in a journal, musical composition, construction with clay or other mediums) serve as positive expressions for anger. Engaging students in group discussions that focus on how each handles feelings of anger can assist students in knowing they are not alone in their reactions and may provide examples for positively and constructively dealing with anger.

Depression Stage. Varied behaviors ranging from crying, lethargy, and withdrawal to avoidance behaviors can indicate depression. For instance, during this stage, students tend to become class clowns and engage in self-destructive behaviors like substance abuse and/or promiscuity.

Praise and nurturing are essential aspects of the recovery process. Frequent reminders that conditions will improve are also helpful (Brammer, 1993). Even a hug or a pat on the back can let the individual know that someone cares. One of the most beneficial activities is to get the individual involved in helping others–such activity tends to bolster self-esteem and put the individual in control over at least some events in his or her life.

Reorganization Stage. Most individuals progress through each of the stages just summarized within a few weeks. Some, however, are unwilling to move out of grieving for fear they will forget the individual who has died or who is no longer a part of their lives. These individuals tend to think that they need permission to continue living from a trusted person such as a family member, friend, and teacher.

One means of assisting the individual to get over this reorganization hump is to suggest a ritual of farewell to end the grieving period. While the ritual must be designed by the mourning individual, suggestions for the ritual can be provided (e.g., a conversation with the deceased, a permanent tribute to the individual such as a monument, a creation of an artistic work or musical composition). Some individuals can finalize this goodbye rather quickly. Others may need several weeks or months before this ritual closure can occur.

Grief counseling is an additional avenue which should be considered to assist one or more students to progress through mourning. Well-prepared professionals such as school counselors, school psychologists, and school social workers can be asked to assist a student in need of grief counseling. In large-scale tragedies (e.g., a natural disaster affecting the whole school), additional community resources (e.g., mental health) may need to be called upon to provide large-scale support and counseling to faculty, staff, and students before the academic schedule is resumed. Petersen and Straub (1992) provide a brief summary of age-specific activities which could be employed to assist students of varying age levels to work through the grieving process. A sample for each age level is provided next:

- *Primary Students.* Put a sad/smiley face on a flipchart and ask students to describe which feeling is associated with the face, recollect a time when they may have felt this way, and share what made them feel better.

- *Middle Level Students.* Discuss the word "grief" before a loss actually occurs. Have students provide examples of events that promote feelings of grief, describe how a person who is grieving feels, and identify ways that a person who is grieving can work through the grief process.

- *Secondary Students.* Discuss different types of loss (e.g., death, divorce, and boy/girlfriend break-up), reactions students may have experienced with regard to the loss and ways of dealing with it.

On the whole, the crisis intervention team must provide support in cases of sudden death, suicide, or other tragic events involving a student or staff member. See Figures 4.1 and 4.2 for different crisis-management plans. Death-related crises linger on, sometimes longer than individuals and schools can handle. However, a memorial service is one way to put closure to such crises. As noted earlier, some deaths (e.g., suicide) might be better dealt with without media-hyped services.

Figure 4.1
CRISIS INTERVENTION PLAN

> The purpose of the crisis team is to provide direction, support, coordination of resources, and effective communication to the students, staff, and community following the sudden death, suicide, or other tragic event involving a student or staff member.

1.   Following the tragic event, the information is funneled to the principal who is the team leader. The principal then gathers as much information as possible. This is accomplished by speaking with the authorities (police, medical examiner, students, friends, etc.). In some instances it is appropriate to speak with the family of the victim.

2.   As soon as this information is gathered a statement is prepared which contains as many *facts* as are available at the time. This statement is typed out and referred to any time the event is being discussed. If this is during the school day, the principal's secretary will prepare the copy.

3.   Immediately after this is prepared the principal notifies the superintendent and the district P.R. person. They are given the exact statement that has been prepared. At that time a decision is made by the team leader if the P.R. person should be asked to come to the school building to help coordinate communication with the media. This determination is made based on the magnitude of the event.

Figure 4.1, *Continued*

4. The crisis team is assembled at this point and informed of the event. If school is not in session, notification is made by phone.

5. It is imperative that the entire staff be informed as soon as possible. If the initial notification comes during the school day, a staff meeting (including the entire adult population of the school) must be called for the end of the day. In the event the notification comes after the staff has left, or when at night, or over a weekend, then the team will implement the phone tree.

6. Every department, certified and classified, must have a phone tree set up for the sharing of information. Each member of the crisis team will be responsible for starting a portion of the phone tree. There will also be a back up list if someone at the base of the tree cannot be reached. All administrators will be involved in this aspect of the plan. When the leader informs the team of the details of the event as he knows them each member will be directed to write down the details. In this way they will refer to these facts as the tree functions. *Each person will be encouraged to write the details also in order to insure the accuracy of the information throughout the communication.*

7. The principal will also include the leadership of the parent organizations as part of the phone tree.

8. At this point all staff members will be notified of an early morning faculty/staff meeting prior to the first day back to school following the event.

Continued on next page.

Figure 4.1, *Continued*

9. Should the event be the suicide of a student, the principal will notify the teachers of the victim personally prior to making any statement in a full faculty meeting.

10. The crisis team will meet as soon as possible for the purpose of planning the school's response to the event. This will include the schedule of events to take place (i.e., meetings). The notification of pertinent community resources including local mental health providers (hospitals & private practitioners, youth ministers, parent and booster groups).

11. Crisis Team Assignments will be made in the following areas:

    •   Contact with the Victim's Family–Principal

    •   Logistics–Principal's Secretary, District Public Relations Person

    •   Staff–Special Education Department Coordinator, Designated Teacher

    •   Victim's Teachers–Psychologist, Principal

    •   Students–Nurse, Designated Student, Counseling Department Coordinator, Psychologist

    •   Parents–Principal

    •   Media–District Public Relations Person, Principal

12. The team must meet again to assess additional support needed, and determine follow-up activities.

Figure 4.2
CRISIS INTERVENTION PLAN FOR DEATH
OCCURRING DURING SCHOOL TIME

Student or Staff Member Accident • Heart Attack • Suicide

1. Summon emergency help–call 911, if necessary.
2. Take action to prevent further deaths.
3. Isolate area where death occurred.
4. Move those who witnessed death to a central holding area.
5. Arrange for notification of next of kin.
6. Notify central office and necessary staff.
7. Notify support staff needed to assist witnesses.
8. Make arrangements for witnesses to receive needed support or be released.
9. Appoint a staff member to meet and stay with family members to see to their comfort while they are in the building.
10. Determine if there are others such as close friends who should be notified.
11. Determine if there is a need to change the schedule or location of a class.
12. Determine if there is a need for class coverage for reassigned staff.
13. Determine the time and method for communicating about the death to the remaining staff, students, and public.
14. Arrange for traffic control around school.
15. Determine plans for remainder of day/week.
16. Establish follow-up of staff and students who were affected by the death.
17. Communicate appropriate memorials to funeral home.

Memorial Service

Whenever a student, faculty, or staff member dies, allowing students to attend the memorial service or planning a memorial service on school grounds can promote healing. Students should be prepared prior to the service and debriefed after the service, especially since many students have never attended a memorial service. Prior to the memorial service, a description of what will take place, possible emotional reactions, and appropriate things to say and do throughout the service will equip students to understand the experience.

After the service, students may have questions about the service, their own reaction, or the actions of others. To aid in the healing process, general and special educators should provide students with opportunities to discuss these questions and vent their emotions. If the dead person was a popular student, teacher, or staff member, a memorial service may be conducted at school. However, no one should be forced to attend the service, so an alternative (e.g., study hall, media center time) should be scheduled for those not wishing to participate. Involving students and staff closest to the deceased in the memorial service may assist them to work collaboratively through the grieving process.

PERSPECTIVES

Death affects the student body, the staff, and the faculty in many ways depending upon who died, how the person died, and what role he or she had in the school community. Death affects students differently, depending upon their developmental stages. Younger children are not as affected as older youth, but all experience some reaction to the loss. It is most helpful when students can discuss their feelings and reactions to death.

Suicide has increased over the last 40 years, and it creates serious problems for all students, parents, and school personnel. People need to be aware of characteristics that may lead to suicide so preventive measures can be taken. It is important to note that people go through various stages when confronted with death. These may last a short time to weeks and even months in some cases. Intervention strategies must be implemented, especially when a student displays emotions such as hostility, depression, or erratic behaviors. When a student displays fear, assurance must be provided. When a student displays anger, it must be diverted into constructive activity. Depressed students must receive positive support. By going through rituals or even grief counseling, lives of persons enduring death-related crises may be positively reorganized.

DISCUSSION QUESTIONS

1. Describe typical death-reaction behaviors that may be observed at the development level of the children or youth you work with.

2. Describe behaviors that may indicate the potential for a student suicide.

3. Describe resources available in your school, district, and community to assist a student who may be contemplating suicide.

4. Assume that a student you deal with has a terminal illness. Briefly summarize the discussion you will have with students about the illness.

5. Prepare a description for your students of what to expect at a memorial service for a classmate who has died. Assume the service will take place at a mortuary and that it will be an open-casket service.

CHAPTER 5

Preparing General and Special Educators For Crises

In an ideal world, people would always benefit from a difficult situation and turn it to some personal gain. However, to categorically assume that a person will emerge renewed from a crisis is naive and ignores the reality of what life crises can do to a person. I do not believe that every life crisis offers a challenge or an opportunity for positive growth experience, a chance to emerge a better and stronger person. In the real world, an event may leave a person changed in ways that could only be construed as adverse. A person's failure to gain strength from such an event reflects the reality of personal experience, not some problem in the attitude or perspective of the person. ... For some people, life becomes "like a lasting storm." (Holmes, 1994, p. ix)

As Holmes's statement indicates, life crises can have adverse effects on people. Consequently, crises require thorough preparation and discipline on the part of general and special educators so that warning signs of crises can be identified and program modifications addressing students' well-being can be made. Students encountering, both currently and in the past, crises related to disruption, disaster, and death demonstrate certain warning signs; these signs and their significance should be incorporated in preservice and inservice materials for general and special educators. Teacher education programs and school districts must not take any crisis situation for granted. Morgan (1994) identified warning signs pertinent to disruption, disaster, and death. These signs include

1. Inability to concentrate.

2. Chronic absenteeism.

3. Poor grades and/or neglect of homework.

4. Poor scores on standardized tests not related to intelligence quotient or learning disabilities.

5. Uncooperative and quarrelsome behavior.

6. Sudden behavior changes.

7. Shy and withdrawn demeanor.

8. Compulsive behaviors.

9. Chronic health problems.

10. Signs of neglect and abuse.

11. Low self-esteem.

12. Anger, anxiety, and/or depression.

13. Poor coping skills.

14. Unnecessary fearfulness.

15. Difficulty adjusting to change.

These "red flags" frequently lead to learned helplessness or the "victim" mentality. To address this issue, one of this book's authors and a colleague (Obiakor, 1994, Obiakor & Weaver, 1995) developed a Comprehensive Support Model (CSM) for preparing general and special educators. The CSM connects the "self," home, and schools with communities to provide opportunities and choices for at-risk students. It highlights a team approach in solving students' problems and puts into practical use the African proverb: It takes a whole village to raise a child. Teacher preparation programs must emphasize the role of families, schools, and communities in the "empowerment" phenomenon: Families, schools, and communities must be empowered to engage in partnership and teamwork in addressing students' crisis situations (Clinton, 1996).

The CSM model is the major thrust of this book. We propose that to effectively deal with disruption, disaster, and death, preservice and inservice programs must focus on rethinking how general and special educators are prepared to identify, assess, categorize, place, and teach students in crises. We advocate necessary paradigm and power shifts so that some of the courses required for graduation in teacher preparation programs include how to motivate professionals to search for "new" meanings. It is absolutely necessary that graduates become aware of crisis intervention information centers located all over the nation. These centers provide critical resources for students, teachers, administrators, and parents. See Table 5.1 for some centers, functions, and phone numbers. Most centers do not give out addresses because of confidentiality and safety considerations for workers and clients.

Disruption, disaster, and death can be overwhelming; therefore, dealing with crisis situations in any one or more of these areas demands complex multidimensional strategies which should be included in teacher preparation programs. In recounting his traumatic experiences in a Nazi concentration camp, Frankl (1985) wrote:

> What was really needed was a fundamental change in our attitude toward life. We had to learn ourselves, and, furthermore, we had to teach the despairing men, that it did not really matter what we expected from life, but rather what life expected from us. We needed to stop asking about the meaning of life, and instead to think of ourselves as those who were being questioned by life—daily and hourly. Our answer must consist, not in talk and meditation, but in right action and in right conduct. Life ultimately means taking the responsibility to find the right answer to its problems and to fulfill the tasks which it constantly sets for each individual. (p. 98)

Frankl's statement demonstrates the need for fundamental changes when a crisis strikes. General and special educators need to be prepared to ameliorate stressors associated with disruption, disaster, and death. To a large extent, preservice and inservice programs must be reformed if they are to effectively equip professionals with innovative crisis-intervention techniques. Programs must offer courses, workshops, or seminars that provide skills in (a) consultation, collaboration and cooperation; (b) interventions specific to student developmental stages; (c) operationalizing student self-concept; and (d) problem solving and/or conflict resolution.

Course on Consultation, Collaboration, and Cooperation

In crisis situations, a team approach to problem solving is of paramount importance. Not only is a team of skilled general and special educators needed, the collaboration and cooperation of this team with parents/guardians is also

Table 5.1
CRISIS INTERVENTION INFORMATION CENTERS

Center	Function	Phone Number
American Academy of Child and Adolescence Psychiatry	Publishes fact sheets for teachers and service providers working with children in crises	(202)966-7300
American Humane Association	Provides resources—including many free publications—on all types of child abuse and neglect	(303)792-9900
Center for Children of Alcoholics	Provides counseling programs for family alcoholic problems	(908)530-8513
Childhelp, USA	Provides comprehensive counseling by professionals working with abused and neglected children and youth	(800)422-4453
Children in Danger Resource Center (Erikson Institute)	Publishes materials for children and youth in crises	(312)755-2250
Families Anonymous	Offers useful programs for concerned parents of youths with drug abuse or other self-destructive behaviors	(800)736-9805
Family Service America	Offers materials for families in crises (e.g., divorce, marriage, stepfamilies, single parents, and aging).	(800)221-2681
Kids Peace (The National Center for Kids in Crisis)	Offers a variety of services and materials for children, parents, and professionals	(800)334-4KID; (800)25-PEACE

Table 5.1, *Continued*

Center	Function	Phone Number
National Association of Community Health Centers	Offers local referrals to people in crises	(202)883-9280
National Center for Missing and Exploited Children	Reports missing children, sightings of missing children, or cases of child pornography	(800)843-5678
National Center on Child Abuse and Neglect in the Administration for Children, Youth and Families	Act as a clearinghouse for child-abuse information	(800)FYI-3366
National Committee for the Prevention of Child Abuse	Provides books, pamphlets, and other information on child abuse	(312)663-3520
National Mental Health Association	Refers callers to centers across the country for information regarding types of mental illness	(703)684-7722
National Runaway Switchboard	Provides crisis counseling information, referral, and services to runaway and homeless youths and families	(800)621-4000
Regional Centers for Drug-Free Schools and Communities	Act as clearinghouses for drug-free schools and communities	(516)589-7022 (Northeast); (800)621-SERC (Southeast); (800)356-2735 (Midwest); (800)234-7972 (Southwest); (800)547-6339 (West)

required (Morgan, 1994). Professionals must be prepared to empower parents through conferencing and meetings (Simpson, 1996), through which parents become partners in fostering skills in

1. Self-control and self-responsibility.
2. Problem solving.
3. Advocacy.
4. Consultation, collaboration, and cooperation.
5. Conflict resolution.
6. Communication.

Crisis management, if it is to be effective, cannot be separated from the more traditional, academic components of the curriculum nor can it be divorced from the community at large. General and special educators must be creative in developing crisis-intervention techniques that combine their needs with those of students, parents, administrators, and other professionals. In short, they must be educated to be "New American Teachers" as outlined by the American Association of State Colleges and Universities (AASCU, 1992):

> It is unlikely that students will have only one teacher. Instead, teaching teams will exist, led by a master teacher, with several levels of skill and specialties represented on the team. The teachers will be scholars, discipline based, and motivated by inquiry. These teacher-scholars will be practitioners well versed in pedagogy, child development, cognitive development, affective skills and subject disciplines. The teachers also will demonstrate a love for learning, and perhaps most of all, a caring for students. Knowledge of cultures, living conditions, family issues, societal issues and the structure of various disciplines will be essential. Members of the teaching team in the New American School will be skilled in techniques of team building and will realize team building is essential both inside and outside the school. They will be skilled in assessment, diagnostic and prescriptive evaluation, and aware of the array of resources available to help students participate in learning. They will know about child development, cognitive development, child psychology, group dynamics, cooperative learning and the effective use of technology. Teachers will know the different learning styles of the diverse body of students found in their classrooms and will be able to deal with issues of gender, race, physical disability and others. (p. 5)

Course on Interventions Specific to Student Developmental Stages

To speed up the healing process, each crisis situation must be dealt with in terms of the specific area and developmental stage of those involved. General and special educators must be prepared to assess each crisis situation differently. Bradley (1988) and Brookes (1991) both explain developmental intervention as a process characterized by stages arranged in a sequence from simple to complex. This technique has been very popular in counseling (Hayes & Aubrey, 1988). General and special educators must be aggressively prepared to know how to utilize innovative developmental intervention strategies. Following are assumptions embedded in developmental intervention:

1. The student is personally involved.
2. The student experiences novel, challenging situations.
3. The student experiences some degree of support and becomes a part of the network of interpersonal relationships.
4. The student perceives structured strategies to tackle problems.
5. The student receives relevant information about his or her performance.
6. The student tests out or applies new acquired attitudes.
7. The student integrates total learning in a reflective atmosphere.

Holmes (1994) indicated that "successful intervention depends on two factors: an appropriate therapeutic attitude and flexibility in choosing and using methods of helping" (p. 43). The multifaceted nature of disruption, disaster, and death must influence the multidimensional preparation of teachers. The traditional "one-size-fits-all" preparation is unworkable. Different crisis situations necessitate different helping situations: Each problem situation must be identified and the length of the helping process and the success of the intervention critically analyzed. Helpers (in this case, general and special education teachers) must be trained to understand the specific-developmental-area nature of a crisis situation. Holmes explained:

> Most helpers do not feel the need to develop a comprehensive theory to explain depression over the death of a spouse, parent, or child. They do not spend a great deal of time developing theoretical explanations of why a

person wants to live in a home, go to the grocery store, or talk to a friend. Some emotions, thoughts, and behaviors simply do not require further explanation. Nor is it necessary when treating real-life problems to develop a psychological interpretation of why a person is saddened, angry, guilt ridden, or worried. There is no need for a psychological theory to explain why the problem will not go away. The causes, reactions, and longevity are obvious. ...In the case of lasting real-life problems, it is certain that there will be no resolution; thus there can be no definable end-point to helping. Helpers who work with chronic serious psychological disorders, including the distress associated with real-life problems, recognize the need for prolonged intervention. (pp. 44, 45)

Course on Operationalizing Student Self-Concepts

There is no doubt that disruption, disaster, and death occur in different dimensions. Problems of broken homes, child abuse, drugs, teenage pregnancy, poverty, school dropouts, low academic performance, and suicide afflict today's youth in increasing numbers. Yet general and special educators sometimes appear ill-prepared or unprepared to confront these problems. Even though these problems affect self-knowledge, self-esteem, and self-ideal, most teachers graduate from teacher education programs without taking courses on self-concepts. This should not come as a surprise because most school reform programs focus on "excellence" in education with little or no respect for issues pertinent to self-concepts. General and special educators must be trained to know how to enhance self-concepts. A few years ago, Borba (1989) developed a K-8 self-esteem curriculum for improving student achievement and behavior and school climate. Teacher education programs must infuse self-understanding and self-enhancement programs into their curricula. As Borba pointed out,

> As a child grows and has more experiences, his/her inner picture of self expands. This inner picture comprises all the descriptions an individual attaches to himself/herself and is called self concept. All of the five components of the self — Security, Selfhood, Affiliation, Mission and Competence — serve to mold the student's inner portrait, which is subjective and therefore not necessarily the same as how another perceives him/her. (p. 5)

It is evident that general and special educators are esteem builders. Therefore, to deal with disruption, disaster, and death, general and special education preparation programs must prepare teachers to know how to increase students' security, selfhood, affiliation, mission, and competence. Based on Borba's (1989) Building Blocks of Self-Esteem, *students' security* can be improved by (a) building a trusting relationship, (b) setting reasonable limits and rules, and (c) creating a caring environment. *Students' selfhood* can be improved by (a) reinforcing more accurate self-descriptions, (b) building on unique abilities, and (c) enhancing ability to express emotions and attitudes. *Students' affiliation* can be improved by (a) promoting inclusion, (b) providing opportunities for self-discovery, and (c) encouraging peer approval and support. *Students' mission* can be improved by (a) enhancing decision-making abilities, (b) charting academic and behavioral performances, and (c) teaching successful goal-setting steps. And *students' competence* can be improved by (a) providing opportunities for increasing individual competencies, (b) providing feedback, and (c) teaching self-praise for accomplishments.

Teacher preparation programs must emphasize that Borba's Building Blocks of Self-Esteem or similar concepts can assist students in dealing with disruption, disaster, and death. Preservice and inservice preparation must incorporate courses, workshops, or seminars on self-concepts. To this end, general and special educators must be knowledgeable on how to

1. Change a student's self-opinion for the better.
2. Influence a student's self-esteem.
3. Develop a sincere concern for the student.
4. Generate a personal rapport with the student.
5. Recognize positive qualities of each individual.
6. Believe that a student's self-image can change.
7. Communicate a student's strengths to him or her.
8. Open up to students by sharing genuine personal qualities.
9. Build a trusting relationship with students.
10. Devote effort and time to help students feel better.
11. Review their self-images periodically.
12. Become a student's role model.

Course on Problem Solving and Conflict Resolution

It appears that some of today's youth lack skills in problem solving, conflict resolution, critical thinking, creative thinking, and abstract thinking. It is no wonder that gang-related and other senseless crimes (e.g., the bombing of Oklahoma Federal Building) are rampant. Interestingly, most teacher preparation programs do not have *specific* courses that deal with these skills. While the focus of most school programs has been on higher standardized test scores, the "victim" mentality has increased, and desperate people have continued to engage in outrageous behaviors (Obiakor, 1996; Obiakor & Weaver, 1995; O'Brien, 1991). According to O'Brien,

> Parents trying to raise respectful children today, unfortunately, have to do it in a disrespectful world. Brutal and hostile acts are shown in nightly television, profane, vulgar and irreverent language is used routinely in the media; greed and selfishness are revealed in important and prominent people, role models are too outrageous or too perfect to be taken seriously. (p. 183)

A logical extension is that general and special educators, administrators, service providers, and parents need to rethink their interpretation of "quality." In teacher preparation programs, problem solving and creative thinking must be integral parts of quality education. In fact, quality education must entail *maximum* learning in teacher education programs. All teachers must be prepared to deal with life imperfections and realities. Problem solving and conflict resolution must be addressed in organizations, programs, and classrooms. It is dangerously deceptive to prepare general and special educators for a puritanic, Utopian society that does not exist. Rather, problem-solving skills must be taught from preschool through university levels. To effectively deal with disruption, disaster, and death, general and special educators must be prepared to refrain from labeling, categorizing, stereotyping, and stigmatizing students (Obiakor, 1996). They must be properly prepared with problem-solving methods such as Dambrowsky's (1983) six-step process:

1. Define the problem by asking questions such as
   a. How do I feel?
   b. Whose problem is this?
   c. Can I do anything?

2. Identify solutions and their consequences.

3. Choose one solution.

4. Make a plan to carry out solution.

5. Try the plan.

6. Evaluate the plan.

PERSPECTIVES

No preparation or training is a panacea for eradicating all the problems confronting today's citizenry. Brookes (1991) confirmed that "to understand more clearly how our students feel, it's helpful to look at our own reactions when placed in a situation where we might make a mistake" (p. 93). It is not easy to intervene in (or eradicate) crisis situations. For general and special educators to avoid potential problems in dealing with disruption, disaster, and death, they must be aggressively prepared to avoid (a) making unwarranted psychopathological interpretations, (b) using theory to control the intervention process, (c) assuming a particular technique is best, (d) judging by usual standards, (e) forcing the issue, (f) taking away protective defenses, (g) offering unrealistic hope, (h) using cliches and platitudes, (i) making misguided expressions of empathy, (j) giving impossible advice, (k) employing pop psychology, and (l) expecting a smooth therapeutic course (Holmes, 1994). Preservice and inservice preparations in general and special education programs must incorporate courses or seminars on consultation, collaboration, and partnership with parents and community resource personnel if problems confronting students are to be solved. Morgan (1994) concluded:

> The problems we face as professionals and as a society dictate that we learn to work together, to use one another's expertise, to trust and depend upon one another, to give some of ourselves to each other, and to give away some of our treasured skills we have been trying to hoard. There is no way that we are going to be successful in our attempts to help children if energies, talents, and information are not pooled. Success in major prevention efforts will never come about until the entire community of professionals, from the bottom up, learns the value of being a team of mental health professionals and not just a team of counselors, a team of teachers, a team of social workers, or a team of psychologists. (p. 232)

DISCUSSION QUESTIONS

1. How could the Comprehensive Support Model (CSM) be used in your setting to help in managing disruption, disaster, and death?

2. How could parents be empowered to help deal with crisis events in your school or community?

3. Briefly discuss strategies to enhance self-concepts of students experiencing crises related to disruption, disaster, and death.

4. Identify *four* courses that could be the main foci of the preparation of future teachers in this day and age. In your opinion, briefly discuss four major objectives that can be incorporated into these courses.

5. If you are invited by your local Board of Education to share your thoughts on workshops and seminars on crisis intervention, which major ideas will you highlight?

EPILOGUE

No one can be totally protected from disruption, disaster, and death. Three years ago, my family faced a crisis resulting from violence. This prompted my cousin (Dr. Darlene Clark-Hine, John A. Hannah Professor of American History, Michigan State University) to express her outrage in the *Chicago Sun Times*. Below is an excerpt that captured my imagination:

> The killing of young black males became an in-my-face issue on September 19, 1992, when my 15- and 17-year-old nephews were shot in the side and in the knee respectively while standing in the doorway of a friend's house across the street from their own home on the south side of Chicago. They had refused to join the local neighborhood gang. The family decided that to save them and avoid further bloodshed the nephews had to be relocated, thus irrevocably transforming the lives of the family members. As a university professor I understand intellectually the crisis, but I considered myself far removed from the killing fields. Silence and inaction I can no longer afford.

Dr. Clark-Hine's outcry is the outcry of most parents and teachers today. Is it any surprise that "things are out of control," "schools must do more," and "schools cannot do everything" are phrases heard in school districts and communities nationwide regarding the myriad of daily and/or episodic crises confronted by today's children and youth? While these comments tend to be more pronounced in urban areas, suburban and rural areas are not immune. As Obiakor, Mehring, and Schwenn have described in this book, multidimensional crises which seep into the school environment and inhibit productive teaching and learning range from various forms of child abuse; death or loss of loved ones; the devastating consequences of low self-esteem and feelings of hopelessness (e.g., violence, homicide, suicide, substance abuse, and teen pregnancy), to unexpected natural disasters.

Crises that result from disruption, disaster, and death are not new phenomena: however, the nature, degree, frequency, and duration of these crises
today occur at a startling rate. Present crises require the concentrated energy
and talents of all who are concerned with improving the quality of life for
children and youth, and ultimately society. Regrettably, in too many school
districts, intervention strategies are almost "invisible," and when they are vis-
ible, they are not in depth enough. Whenever a crisis occurs, both learners
and school personnel are placed in at-risk situations (Obiakor & Algozzine,
1995).

Children and youth, frustrated and frightened, tend to respond in overt
and subtle ways through their absenteeism, poor school performances, and
inappropriate social behaviors. Their frustration results in statements like "Who
cares?" "Why should I try?" Public education is not expected to solve all soci-
etal problems. But, school personnel cannot allow crises to be impediments
toward a healthy school culture that can help all students to maximize their
potential. In other words, current and future schools must be restructured and
reorganized such that systematic and appropriate attention is given to students' crises while concurrently exposing students to effective educational
services.

In this book, Obiakor, Mehring, and Schwenn are correct in suggesting
that collaborative networks between school and community agencies (such as
the Comprehensive Support Model) should be made available to assist schools
in pragmatically addressing crises without sacrificing academic-oriented services. I strongly believe that forging collaborative networks with grassroot
and other significant organizations and resources within the communities offers significant advantages to school personnel and students. I concur with the
authors that school personnel must become knowledgeable about valid resources which may otherwise go unnoticed. Such resources can be included
within the school's comprehensive strategic plans to equip general and special educators with tools to combat crises.

Additionally, including resources found within the school's community
establishes the framework for authentic school-community shared responsibilities. Educators can share information regarding these resources with parents through teacher conferences, special parent-school meetings, and/or the

school's newsletter or handbook. These inclusive actions will enhance the school's role as a liaison or advocate for appropriate services for children and families requiring help. Parental involvement is often an integral component of programs provided by grassroot organizations. As a result, collaborative linkages with these vital resources provide the school with yet another mechanism to recruit parents and significant others as empowered participatory members.

It is common knowledge that the majority of administrators, educators, and other school professionals do not live in the communities of the students they serve. Thus, while school personnel can empathize and understand, to a degree, crises experienced by students, a realistic, concrete comprehension of the daily stress confronted by students may be difficult. To meaningfully intervene in crises impacting students at risk, it is imperative that schools go beyond the traditional public service, social, and health agencies.

In doing so, outreach initiatives by individual schools must seek to establish and maintain authentic collaborative or consultative relationships with significant individuals and organizations which provide invaluable services to local families and youth. These resources may include respected community and church leaders; service fraternities and sororities; professional organizations; grass root organizations; and civic, service, and social organizations (Ascher, 1993; Ford, 1995; Obiakor, 1994). These kinds of resources and organizations can offer a variety of ongoing programs to foster the healthy development of families and youth.

As Obiakor, Mehring, and Schwenn point out in this book, these ongoing programs should include

1. Academic tutoring.

2. Workshops on self-esteem, positive decision making, goal setting, life-survival skills, and dealing with conflicting or stressful situations (e.g., school conflicts, gangs, sexism, and racism).

3. Special fairs on health issues (e.g., alcohol and drugs, teen sexuality and pregnancy, sexual diseases, and environmental concerns).

4. Gender-specific programs (e.g., Rites of Passage programs for females and males).

No doubt, this book is a much needed text in general and special education. It has successfully addressed appropriate crisis-intervention strategies for dealing with disruption, disaster, and death. No one can be totally protected from crises. However, with constructive collaborative, consultative, and cooperative techniques, we can minimize and almost eradicate the pressures of crises on students, parents, teachers, administrators, and service providers.

Bridgie Alexis Ford
Professor of Special Education
University of Akron

REFERENCES

American Association of State Colleges and Universities. (1992). *Teacher education for the twenty-first century.* Washington, DC: Author.

Ascher, C. (1993). *Changing schools for urban students: The school development program, accelerated schools, and success for all* (Trends and Issues No.18). New York: ERIC Clearinghouse on Urban Education, Institute for Urban and Minority Education.

Berdine, W. H., & Blackhurst, A. E. (1985). *An introduction to special education.* Boston: Little, Brown.

Berk, L. E. (1991). *Child development* (2nd ed.). Boston: Allyn & Bacon.

Blumenthal, S. (1990, December 26). Youth suicide: The physician's role in suicide prevention. *Journal of The American Medical Association, 264,* 3194-3196.

Borba, M. (1989). *Esteem builders: A K-8 self-esteem curriculum for improving student achievement, behavior and school climate.* Rolling Hills Estates, CA: Jalmer Press.

Bradley, L. J. (1988). Developmental assessment: A life-span process. In R. Hayes & R. Aubrey (Eds.), *New directions for counseling and human development* (pp. 136-157). Denver, CO: Love.

Brammer, L. M. (1993). *The helping relationship: Process and skills* (5th ed.). Boston: Allyn & Bacon.

Brookes, R. (1991). *The self-esteem teacher.* Circle Pines, MN: American Guidance Service.

Brumback, R., Statton, R., & Wilson, H. (1980). Neuropsychological study of children during and after remission of endogenous depressive episodes. *Perceptual and Motor Skills, 50,* 1163-1167.

Children's Defense Fund. (1994). *The state of America's children yearbook.* Minneapolis, MN: Author.

Clark-Stewart, A., & Friedman, S. (1987). *Child development: Infancy through adolescence.* New York: John Wiley.

Clinton, H. R. (1996). *It takes a village and other lessons children teach us.* New York: Simon & Schuster.

Cohen-Sandler, R., Berman, A., & King, R. (1982). Life stress and symptomatology: Determinants of suicidal behavior in children. *Journal of the American Academy of Child Psychiatry, 21,* 178-186.

Comerford, D. L., & Jacobson, M. G. (1987, April). *Suspension–Capital punishment for misdemeanors: The use of suspension at four suburban junior high schools and viable alternatives that could work.* Paper presented at the annual meeting of the American Educational Research Association, Washington, D.C.

Cornell, J. (1982). The great international disaster book (3rd ed.). New York: Charles Scribner's Sons.

Dembrowsky, C. H. (1983). *Affective skill development for adolescents: Teacher's Manual.*

Cincinnati, OH: Special Education Instruction Resource Project.

Dyer, J., & Kreitman, N. (1984). Hopelessness, depression, and suicidal intent. *British Journal of Psychiatry, 144*, 127-133.

Eggen, P., & Kauchak, D. (1994). *Educational psychology* (2nd ed.). New York: Merrill/ Macmillan.

Ford, B. A. (1995). African American community involvement processes and special education: Essential networks for quality programs. In B. A. Ford, F. E. Obiakor, & J. M. Patton (Eds.), *Effective education of African American exceptional learners: New perspectives* (pp.235-272). Austin, TX: Pro-Ed.

Forness, S. (1988). School characteristics of children and adolescents with depression. In R. B. Rutherford, C. M. Nelson, & S. R. Forness (Eds.), *Bases of severe behavior disorders of children and youth* (pp. 177-204). Boston: Little, Brown.

Frankl, V. E. (1985). *Man's search for new meaning.* New York: Washington Square Press.

Gargiulo, R. M. (1985). *Working with parents of exceptional children: A guide for professionals.* Boston: Houghton Mifflin.

Goldstein, A. P., Harootunian, B., & Conoley, J. C. (1994). *Student aggression: Prevention, management, and replacement training.* New York: Guilford Press.

Gordon, S. (1985). *When living hurts.* New York: Union of Hebrew Congregations.

Gronsnickle, D. R., & Stephens, R. D. (1992). *Developing personal and social responsibility: A guide for community action.* Malibu, CA: National School Safety Center.

Guetzloe, E. (1989). *Youth suicide: What the educator should know.* Reston, VA: Council for Exceptional Children.

Guetzloe, E. (1991). *Depression and suicide: Special education students at risk.* Reston, VA: Council for Exceptional Children.

Hallahan, D. P., & Kauffman, J. M. (1997). *Exceptional children: Introduction to special education* (7th ed.). Boston: Allyn & Bacon.

Harris, L. (1996). *Between hope and fear: Teens speak out on crime and community.* Washington, DC: National Crime Prevention Council and The National Institute for Citizen Education in the Law.

Hayes, R., & Aubrey, R. (1988). *New directions for counseling and human development.* Denver, CO: Love.

Heward, W. L. (1996). *Exceptional children: An introduction to special education* (5th ed.). Englewood Cliffs, NJ: Prentice Hall.

Holmes, C. B. (1994). *Like a lasting storm: Helping with real-life problems.* Brandon, VT: Clinical Psychology.

Hughes, A., Clarke, M., DeHotman, S., & Bean, S. (1996, April). *Social, multicultural, and legal perspectives of school violence.* Paper presented at the Council for Exceptional Children International Convention, Orlando, FL.

Johnson, D. W., & Johnson, R. T. (1991). *Teaching students to be peacemakers.* Edina, MN: Interaction Books.

Jones, M., & Patterson, L. (1992). *Preventing chaos in times of crisis: A guide for school administrators.* Los Alamitos, CA: Southwest Regional Laboratory.

Kadel, S., & Follman, J. (1993). *Reducing school violence.* Greensboro, NC: Southeastern Regional Vision for Education.

Kansas City School District. (1993). *Conflict resolution program.* Kansas City, MO: Author.

King, M., & Goldman, R. (1988). Crisis intervention and prevention with children of divorce and remarriage. In J. Sandoval (Ed.), *Crisis counseling, intervention, and prevention in the schools* (pp. 58-71). Hillsdale, NJ: Erlbaum.

Kirk, W. G. (1993). *Adolescent suicide.* Champaign, IL: Research Press.

Kleinfeld, A., & Young, R. (1989). Risk of pregnancy and dropping out of school among special education adolescents. *Journal of Social Health, 59*, 359-361.

Kroth, R. L. (1985). *Communicating with parents of exceptional children.* Denver, CO: Love.

Leder, M. (1987). *Dead serious: A book for teenagers about teenage suicide.* New York: Atheneum.

Leone, P. E. (1991). *Alcohol and other drugs: Use, abuse and disabilities.* Reston, VA: Council for Exceptional Children.

Leviton, S., & Greenstone, J. L. (1989). Intervention procedure. In W. Fowler & J. L. Greenstone (Eds.), *Crisis intervention compendium* (pp. 48-54). Littleton, MA: Copley.

Lindemann, E. (1944). Symptomology and management of acute grief. *American Journal of Psychiatry, 101*, 211-217.

Long, N. (1992). Managing a shooting incident. *Journal of Emotional and Behavioral Problems, 1*, 23-26.

Mattison, R., Humphrey, J., Kales, S., Hernit, R., & Finkenbinder, R. (1986). Psychiatric background and diagnosis of children evaluated for special class placement. *Journal of Child Psychiatry, 25*, 514-520.

Meemot, C., & Stone, A. (1989, June 15). Firearms and youngsters: Deadly, tragic mix. *USA Today,* p. 3A.

Mehring, T. A. (1995). Crisis intervention: A model for behavior management. In F. E. Obiakor & B. Algozzine (Eds.), *Managing problem behaviors: Perspectives for general and special educators* (pp. 136-160). Dubuque, IA: Kendall/Hunt.

Morgan, S. R. (1994). *At-risk youth in crises: A team approach in the schools* (2nd ed.). Austin, TX: Pro-Ed.

Muccigrosso, L., Scavarda, M., Simpson-Brown, R., & Thalacker, B. E. (1991). *Double jeopardy: Pregnant and parenting youth in special education.* Reston, VA: Council for Exceptional Children.

National Education Service Foundation. (1994). *Breaking the cycle of violence: A call for action.* Bloomington, IN: Author.

National School Safety Center. (1990). *School crisis prevention and response.* Malibu, CA: Author.

National School Safety Center. (1993). *Student and staff victimization.* Malibu, CA: Pepperdine University Press.

Obiakor, F. E. (1994). *The eight-step multicultural approach: Learning and teaching with a smile.* Dubuque, IA: Kendall/Hunt.

Obiakor, F. E. (1996, January 24). The power of the word. *The Emporia Gazette,* p. 7.

Obiakor, F. E., & Algozzine, B. (1995). *Managing problem behaviors: Perspectives for general and special educators.* Dubuque, IA: Kendall/Hunt.

Obiakor, F. E., & Weaver, K. A. (1995, May 17). Has U.S. become a nation of victims? *The Emporia Gazette,* p. 7.

O'Brien, S. J. (1991, Spring). How do you raise respectful children in a disrespectful world? *Childhood Education,* pp. 183-184.

O'Rourke, J. (1993). *Conflict mediation and drug free schools.* Topeka, KS: Kansas Children's Service League.

Peck, M. (1985). Crisis intervention treatment with chronically and acutely suicidal adolescents. In M. L. Peck, N. L. Farberow, & R. E. Litman (Eds.), *Youth suicide* (pp. 112-122). New York: Springer.

Petersen, S., & Straub, R. L. (1992). *School crisis survival guide.* West Nyack, NY: Center for Applied Research in Education.

Pfeffer, C. (1981). The distinctive features of children who threaten and commit suicide. In C. F. Wells & I. R. Stuart (Eds.), *Self destructive behavior in children and adolescents* (pp. 106-120). New York: Van Nostrand Reinhold.

Pfeffer, C. (1986). *The suicidal child.* New York: Guilford Press.

Pfeffer, C., & Plutchick, R. (1982). Psycho–pathology of latency-age children: Relation to treatment planning. *Journal of Nervous and Mental Disease, 17,* 193-197.

Pfeffer, C., Zuckerman, S., Plutchick, R., & Mizruchi, M. (1984). Suicidal behavior in normal school children: A comparison with child psychiatric patients. *Journal of the American Academy of Child Psychiatry, 23,* 416-423.

Pitcher, G., & Poland, S. (1993). *Crisis intervention in the schools.* New York: Guilford Press.

Rapp, J. A., Carrington, F., & Nicholson, G. (1992). *School crime and violence: Victim's rights.* Malibu, CA: National School Safety Center.

Riley, R. A. (1993, July). *Curbing youth violence.* Paper presented at the Forum on Youth Violence organized by the National Association of School Psychologists, Washington, DC.

Robbins, D., & Alessi, N. (1985). Depressive symptoms and suicidal behavior in adolescents. *American Journal of Psychiatry, 142,* 588-592.

Rosenthal, P., & Rosenthal, S. (1984). Suicidal behavior by pre-school children. *American Journal of Psychiatry, 141,* 520-525.

Salkind, N. (1990). *Child development.* New York: Holt, Rinehart & Winston.

Schoenfeldt and Associates. (1994). *Crisis response teams for schools and communities.* Foresthill, CA: Author.

Schwenn, J. O. (1994). Serving culturally and linguistically diverse exceptional students in the REI. In A. F. Rotatori, J. O. Schwenn, & F. W. Litton (Eds.), *Advances in special education* (Vol. 8, pp. 53-73). Greenwich, CT: JAI Press.

Sheehy, G. (1976). *Passages: Predictable crises of adult life.* New York: Bantam Books.

Silva, T. (1992, August 16). Does suspending students help or hurt? *Gainsville Sun,* pp. 1A & 4A.

Simpson, R. L. (1996). *Working with parents and families of exceptional children and youth: Techniques for successful conferencing and collaboration* (3rd ed.). Austin, TX: Pro-Ed.

Simpson, R. L., Miles, B. S., Walker, B. L., Ormsbee, C. K., & Downing, J. A. (1991). *Programming for aggressive and violent students.* Reston, VA: Council for Exceptional Children.

Smith, L. A. (1989). A crisis intervention model. In W. R. Fowler & J. L. Greenstone (Eds.), *Crisis intervention compendium* (pp. 4-12). Littleton, MA: Copley.

Staff. (1996, January 12). Violent surroundings harm kids learning, report says. *Education Daily, 28,* 1-2.

Stark, K. (1990). *Childhood depression: School-based intervention.* New York: Guilford Press.

Task Force on School Discipline. (1990). *Report of the task force on school discipline.* Tallahassee, FL: Florida Department of Education.

U.S. Department of Justice. (1986). *Reducing school crime and student misbehavior: A problem-solving strategy.* Washington, DC: National Institute of Justice.

Van Acker, R. (1996). *Types of youth aggression and violence and implications for prevention and treatment.* Reston, VA: Council for Children with Behavior Disorders, Council for Exceptional Children.

Vidal, J. (1986, October). Establishing a suicidal prevention program. *National Association of Secondary School Principals Bulletin*, pp. 68-72.

Webb, N. B. (1991). *Play therapy with children in crisis: A casebook for practitioners.* New York: Guilford Press.

Webb-Johnson, G., Obiakor, F. E., & Algozzine, B. (1995). Self-concept development: An effective tool for behavior management. In F. E. Obiakor & B. Algozzine (Eds.), *Managing problem behaviors: Perspectives for general and special education* (pp. 161-177). Dubuque, IA: Kendall/Hunt.

Wheelock, A. (1986, November). *The way out: Student exclusion practices in Boston middle schools.* Boston: Massachusetts Advocacy Center.

Woolfolk, A. E. (1993). *Educational psychology* (5th ed.). Boston: Allyn & Bacon.

Ysseldyke, J. E., & Algozzine, B. (1995). *Special education* (3rd ed.). Boston: Houghton Mifflin.

About the Authors

Festus E. Obiakor

Festus E. Obiakor, Ph.D., is a Professor of Special Education in the Division of Psychology and Special Education, Emporia State University, Emporia, Kansas. His graduate degrees are from Texas Christian University and New Mexico State University. Dr. Obiakor is a teacher, scholar, consultant, and poet. His specific areas of interest include self-concept, crisis intervention, multicultural education, comparative/international education, retention of at-risk students, and educational reform/program evaluation.

Dr. Obiakor has more than 100 academic publication including books, chapters, monographs, articles, commentaries, essays, and poetry. In November 1992, he edited the historic special issue of *Exceptional Children* that addressed issues in the education of African-American youth in special education settings. He is on the editorial board of more than 10 scholarly journals including *Exceptional Children* and *Multiple Voices* for which he serves as Associate Editor. Dr. Obiakor has served as visiting professor and/or scholar at Hendrix College's Department of English, Indiana University of Pennsylvania's Black Cultural Center, Portland State University's Department of Special Education, and the University of Georgia's Learning Disability and Training Center.

His honors and awards include Horace J. Traylor Minority Leadership Award, Emporia State University Presidential Award for Distinguished Service to Diversity, induction into Psi Chi National Honor Society in Psychology, and Who's Who Among America's Teachers. Not only does Dr. Obiakor believe "it takes a village to raise a child," he also believes "there are multidimensional ways to accomplish this crucial task."

Teresa Mehring

Teresa "Tes" Mehring, Ph.D., is the Dean of the Teachers College at Emporia State University. She is also a professor in the Division of Psychology and Special Education. Her graduate degrees are from the University of Kansas and Southwest Missouri State University. Dr. Mehring is a leader, teacher, scholar, and consultant. Specific areas of interest include crisis intervention, authentic assessment, motivation, and memory. She has more than 40 scholarly publications including books, chapters, monographs, articles, videotapes, and tests. She has presented at more than 100 international, national, and state professional conferences. Dr. Mehring has received funding for grant proposals from more than 20 federal, state, and private agencies. Recent honors and awards include Who's Who Among America's Teachers (1996), Kansas Educator of the Year (1995), The Teachers College Outstanding Research Award (1994), and the Council for Learning Disabilities Professional of the Year Award (1994). Dr. Mehring's philosophy about teaching is best summarized by a Mary Lou Tucker quotation, "There is no vision clearer, no service greater, no profession more dignified, no work more rewarding, than that of providing the best possible opportunity for each student."

John O. Schwenn

John O. Schwenn, Ph.D., is the Associate Vice President for Academic Affairs and Dean of Graduate Studies and Research at Emporia State University. He is also a Professor in the Division of Psychology and Special Education. His graduate degrees are from the University of Wisconsin - Madison. Dr. Schwenn is a teacher, leader, scholar, and consultant. His specific areas of interest include behavior management, crisis intervention, assessment, teaching strategies, and diversity. His 40 scholarly publications include books, chapters, and journal articles. He has presented at more than 60 international, national, and state professional gatherings. Dr. Schwenn is the editor of *Emporia State Research Studies* and is on the editorial board of four other journals including *Exceptional Children.* His recent honors include Who's Who Among America's Teachers (1996) and The Teachers College Outstanding Research Award (1994). Dr. Schwenn believes our future is our children, and we must provide for *all* children's best possible growth and development.

CEC Teacher Resources

Disruption, Disaster, and Death: Helping Students Deal with Crises
by Festus E. Obiakor, Teresa A. Mehring, and John O. Schwenn

This one-of-a-kind resource leads the way in providing a candid look at the problems related to situations that involve disruption, disaster, and death and offers a wide array of resources and practices to help students cope with these events. The content is appropriate for general education, but the book also contains sections on how children with exceptionalities may be specifically affected.

No. P5190, 1997, 120 pp.   ISBN 0-86586-289-3
Regular Price $26.95   CEC Member Price $18.95

Crossover Children: A Sourcebook for Helping Children Who Are Gifted and Learning Disabled, Second Edition *by Marlene Bireley*

A rich resource that provides specific strategies to help children who are gifted and learning disabled and/or ADD control impulsivity, increase attention, enhance memory, improve social skills, and develop a positive self-concept. It also provides recommendations for academic interventions and enrichment activities.

No. P5121, 1995, 94pp.   ISBN 0-86586-264-8
Regular Price $28.00   CEC Member Price $19.60

Back Off, Cool Down, Try Again: Teaching Students How to Control Aggressive Behavior
by Sylvia Rockwell

A vividly descriptive primer on how to nurture the social development of students with aggressive behavior in a classroom setting using the stages of group development as the basis for classroom management. The focus moves from teacher control to control through peer interaction. Strategies for group management, affective and academic instruction, and planning, documentation, and consultation are presented.

No. P5120, 1995, 144pp.   ISBN 0-86586-263-X
Regular Price $27.00   CEC Member Price $19.00

Tough to Reach, Tough to Teach: Students with Behavior Problems *by Sylvia Rockwell*
Through the use of anecdotes, the author prepares teachers for the shock of abusive language and hostile behavior in the classroom. This book will allow you to have a plan for meeting the challenges of teaching these students more effective ways to communicate. Provides many practical management strategies for defusing and redirecting disruptive behavior.

No. P387, 1993, 106pp.   ISBN 0-86586-235-4
Regular Price $24.00   CEC Member Price $16.80

Survival Guide for the First-Year Special Education Teacher, Revised Edition
by Mary Kemper Cohen, Maureen Gale, and Joyce M. Meyer

Tips for new teachers to start you off on the right foot. Tells how to get organized, how to get to know the students, how to get along with co-workers and parents, and how to take care of yourself.

No. P335R, 1994, 48pp.   ISBN 0-86586-256-7
Regular Price $12.00   CEC Member Price $8.40

Assess for Success: Handbook on Transition Assessment *by Patricia L. Sitlington, Deborah A. Neubert, Wynne Begun, Richard C. Lombard, and Pamela J. Leconte*
Helps the IEP team decide what to assess and how assessment data should be collected and used within the context of career development. Case studies illustrate how this concept applies to students with different levels of ability and different career visions. Provides strategies for assessing self-determination skills.

No. P5155, 1996, 136pp.   ISBN 0-86586-281-8
Regular Price $30.00   CEC Member Price $21.00

Prices may change without notice. Send orders to: The Council for Exceptional Children, Dept. K70150, 1920 Association Drive, Reston, VA 20191-1589. 1-800-CEC-READ.